On Your Bike
Cheshire

Sheila Simpson

COUNTRYSIDE BOOKS
NEWBURY, BERKSHIRE

COUNTRYSIDE BOOKS
3 Catherine Road
Newbury, Berkshire

To view our complete range of books,
please visit us at
www.countrysidebooks.co.uk

ISBN 1 85306 778 4

Front cover picture taken in Delamere Forest
Photographs and maps by the author
Designed by Graham Whiteman

Typeset by Textype, Cambridge
Produced through MRM Associates Ltd., Reading
Printed in Italy

CONTENTS

AREA MAP SHOWING THE LOCATIONS OF THE RIDES

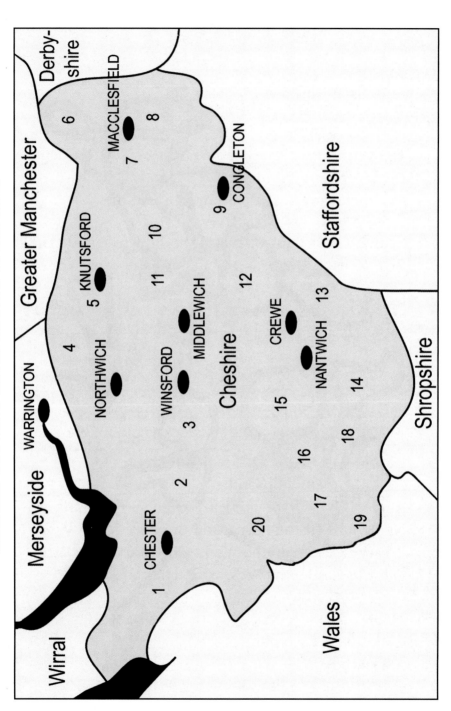

INTRODUCTION

The intricate network of Cheshire lanes offers an almost endless variety of cycle rides, for the most part on the flat or gently rolling Cheshire Plain, and, on most days of the week you will encounter plenty of other cyclists, particularly on the Cheshire Cycleway and Cycle Cheshire circuits which have been signposted by the local authority. This is easy cycling country through farmland and magnificent parkland surrounding the great Cheshire halls, many now open to the public and offering attractions for all ages.

For those seeking drama, the western border, facing Wales, is dotted with fascinating castles, whilst the east encroaches on the Peak District and offers climbs as tough as any in the world. To the south, the county melts imperceptibly into rural North Shropshire but, to the north, Greater Manchester and Merseyside have left an urban legacy of disused railways which now provide off-road cycle routes through towns rich in industrial archaeology. Throughout the county, Cheshire's canal network, now a valuable leisure resource, offers a colourful addition to the scenery in both town and country.

The 20 circular rides in this book have been designed to visit a variety of places of interest. Most routes use country lanes almost exclusively, though some include reasonably surfaced canal towpaths, cycleways and forest trails. The starting venues have been chosen for their ease of access and availability of car parking facilities and, where possible, rail access.

The routes vary in length from 15 to just over 30 miles and, with the help of a map, most can be easily shortened, if required, or linked to neighbouring circuits to give a longer ride. You don't need a special bike to ride in Cheshire, or even to be particularly experienced on two wheels. There are circuits here to suit family groups and those new to cycling as well as those who ride regularly. Only one ride is relentlessly hilly and the need for low gears is mentioned at its start.

There are either cafés or country pubs on all the circuits, usually both, and most proprietors are used to catering for cyclists' appetites. You will find that you need to eat and drink (not too much alcohol though) more than usual when cycling; that's part of the fun.

Sheila Simpson

GUIDE TO USING THIS BOOK

Each route is preceded by details to help you:

The **route title** gives the place where the ride starts plus an overview of the area to be covered on the ride and the total mileage.

The **introduction** provides a brief description of the route and mentions particular features that you will see. The maps cited are all Ordnance Survey maps from the 1:50,000 Landranger series. These particular maps are well worth buying (or most libraries will lend them) as they contain a wealth of detail which will add considerably to your enjoyment.

The **starting point** provides details of how to get to the start from the nearest railway station, or the major through roads, along with a brief indication of where you might park a car. **Places for refreshments** along the route are mentioned, sometimes particular pubs or tearooms but there are others just waiting for you to discover them.

The **note on the terrain** draws your attention to the need for a bike that has really low gears for Route 8 and the first few miles of Route 7. The remaining routes may have the odd steep hill but are almost entirely in flat or gently rolling countryside. You don't need a special bike but, if buying a new machine, remember that it is useful to have low gears in reserve.

THE ROUTES

One of the advantages of using this guide is that the route details refer to what you will see on the road itself. I have personally ridden all of the routes which make up the 20 rides taking note of signposting, the names of roads and identifying visible features to help ensure that those following the routes will not get lost. The rides have been arranged by geographical location as identified in the area map rather than by their relative lengths or the ease or difficulty of the terrain to be encountered.

Route descriptions are kept simple. Instructions to turn left or right are printed in bold: **turn L**, **turn R**. Instructions to continue straight on, or go straight over a crossroads are not in bold.

Each ride is accompanied by a sketch map tracing the suggested route to give you a general idea of directions. More detailed mapping can be found on the recommended Ordnance Survey map.

At the end of each chapter there are brief details of places of interest along the ride. I would advise reading this before embarking on the ride or you may regret what you have missed!

COMFORT AND SAFETY

For your safety on these rides it is important that your bicycle is roadworthy, that you and your companions, if any, are competent bike-handlers, and that you are familiar with the rules of the road.

The routes have been devised to ensure, as far as possible, that busy main roads are avoided. Inevitably I have had to include a few short sections of A or B roads on some routes but these have been kept to a minimum. However, it is important that riders are aware of potential dangers. Wear clothing that is easily seen. Bright colours are best and reflective strips on clothing and/or on a saddlebag are easily visible to other road users in dull conditions. Avoid tight clothing; it should be either loose, without flapping too much, or of a stretchy fabric.

Take waterproofs with you in case of rain. You should also carry some tools: a pump, tyre levers and spare inner tubes are the bare minimum.

I would also advise you to carry some cereal bars or equivalent and a drink, as one can run out of energy very quickly on a bike and just as quickly recover once fed; this applies particularly to children.

It is useful to carry your supplies in a small bag, firmly attached behind the saddle, as a bag on your back can quickly become an annoyance when cycling and can upset your balance.

Very young children can enjoy cycling in a kiddy seat or assisting an adult by pedalling a trailer or tandem. Mine were in a kiddy seat before the age of one year, pedalling a trailer at the age of three and on their own bikes at seven, riding trails and roads under supervision. When a child first starts to ride solo, traffic free routes are invaluable places to learn bike handling skills and develop stamina. The accompanying adults will then need to ride behind young children on the lanes, directing them on the road and pointing out any potential hazards well in advance.

Above all enjoy a safe, trouble-free ride and if you follow this advice, should you get a puncture or should it rain, you will be prepared for such eventualities.

The Wirral Way, Chester and Ness Botanic Gardens

27 miles

One of the easiest of rides, with a high proportion of traffic-free, surfaced cycle paths, this is an ideal route for those who like to explore the countryside in a leisurely fashion. The route begins on the Wirral Way and follows the well-signposted National Cycle Route (NCR) 56 onto single-track lanes and bridleways to the tarmac towpath of the Shropshire Union Canal. This links to NCR 5 through Chester, a short section of cycle path through a new estate in Wales, a bridleway back into rural Cheshire and then onto public roads with views of, and visits to, the marshes of the Dee Estuary. Take your binoculars if you are at all interested in wildfowl.

Map: OS Landranger 117, Chester & Wrexham (GR 284779).

Starting point: The Wirral Country Park car park at Parkgate. *By car:* from the A540 between Chester and Hoylake, take the B5134 through Neston. The car park is signposted on the left soon after the Parkgate village sign. *By train:* from nearby Parkgate Station. *By cycle:* from NCR 5 or 56.

Refreshments: There are attractive cafés and pubs in Parkgate, The Yacht pub on the A540, the Eureka, a famous cyclists' café at Two Mills (open at weekends), and Ness Botanic Gardens, which has tea rooms just outside the entrance.

The route: Approximately 14 miles of cycle paths and bridleways, 11 miles of lanes, 1¼ miles of A road and ½ mile of B road.

Leave the car park onto the Wirral Way (by the notice board). The path is lined by mature trees, has a firm crushed stone surface, and there is a separate track for horses. **Turn R** when the trail ends briefly (signposted NCR 56), through the bollards (beware kerb), and follow the road onto the cycleway alongside a one-way road. Over the crossroads, rejoin the trail, which runs first through a deep cutting, with pick marks still to be seen from when the railway was gouged out of the sandstone cliffs by hand, and then out onto an embankment with views over pasture land. Go through a gate and narrow underpass and rejoin the trail through a gate. Continue over a level crossing to Hadlow Road Station, Willaston. This has been

The Wirral Way

restored to its appearance during active life and is worth exploration.

Continue and **turn L** immediately before the bridge over the trail (signposted NCR 56) and very soon **turn R** at the T-junction (signposted NCR 56) onto a lane going over the bridge. **Turn R** on a left-hand bend onto a stony road (signposted NCR 56). Through a bridleway gate the surface becomes smooth concrete and, after the farmyard, there is tarmac. **Turn L** at the T-junction (signposted NCR 56) and soon **turn R** on a left-hand bend (Ledsham Hall Lane – signposted NCR 56). Go over the crossroads and past a British

Nuclear Fuels site which is almost undetectable in its rural setting. **Turn L** at the T-junction and through Capenhurst village. Pass the BNFL main entrance and soon **turn R**, immediately before a bridge (signposted NCR 56). Go straight across a main road to **turn R** onto a cycle path and immediately **turn L** (Coalpit Lane – signposted NCR 56).

Turn L immediately before a bridge and through a gate onto a tarmac path (signposted NCR 56). Soon go through a gate and **turn R** on a stone and tarmac path with a railway on the right. Continue through a tunnel under the M56,

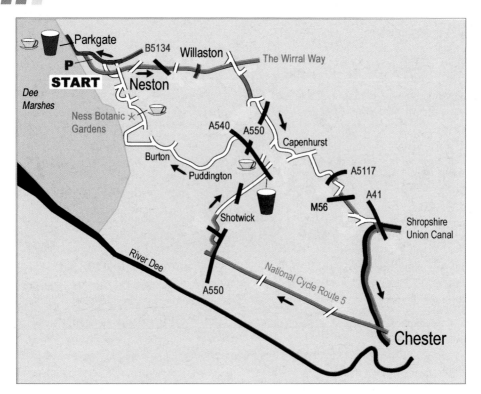

through a gate and straight over a gated crossroads. Go through a final gate and soon **turn L** at a T-junction onto a lane (all signposted NCR 56).

Turn L at a T-junction (signposted NCR 56 and 70, the Cheshire Cycleway). At a main road T-junction, do not cross the road but **turn R** onto the shared cycle/pedestrian facility, cross the bridge, and immediately **turn R** to descend to the canal where you **turn L** onto the towpath.

Follow the towpath to Chester where you go under bridge 128 and immediately **turn L** up the path

(signposted NCR 5). *For a worthwhile detour, remain on the towpath for a further ¾ mile to visit Chester's historic city centre, perhaps leaving your bicycle at the library while you explore on foot. Retrace.* **Turn L** on NCR 5, to go over the canal bridge on an attractive tarmac path which leads out of town through pleasant suburbs and across the border into Wales.

Eventually the trail passes under a major road and crosses a road at a toucan (pedestrian/cycle controlled lights). Immediately after crossing the road, leave NCR 5 **turning R** onto a shared cycle/pedestrian path through a business park. Follow the

Riders on the Shropshire Union Canal towpath

path as it crosses a road to **turn R** at a mini-roundabout. Soon, as the path turns sharp left, **turn R** onto a road (Green Lane West) to pass under a major road. Past some houses on the left, the road becomes a bridleway with a stone/earth surface. Follow this track as the road bends left and over a small stone bridge and the surface becomes a firmer packed stone and rises to a gate into the lovely village of Shotwick. Keep right leaving the village. Go straight over the crossroads (Shotwick Lane) and climb gradually through lovely Shotwick Dale. **Turn L** at the T-junction by the Yacht pub onto the A540 (unsignposted). Approaching traffic lights, note the Eureka Café on the left. Go over the crossroads at the lights and soon **turn L** (signposted Puddington). Go through Puddington and **turn L** at the T-junction in Burton. Leaving Burton, **turn L** (Station Road – signposted Cheshire Cycleway). The road descends to the saltmarshes (an interesting Wildfowler's Walk is described on a notice board). Follow the road up the hill and **turn L** at the T-junction (signposted Cheshire Cycleway) to pass Ness Gardens.

Entering Ness, **turn L** in front of the Wheatsheaf pub (Well Lane – signposted Cheshire Cycleway). **Turn L** at a T-junction (signposted Little Neston). Continue over a mini-roundabout (signposted

Cheshire Cycleway). Go under a railway bridge into Neston and very soon **turn L** (Church Lane) and through a miniature tunnel. **Turn R** at a T-junction and immediately **turn L** at a T-junction (Parkgate Road). To return to Wirral Country Park, **turn L** after the Parkgate town sign, but I recommend continuing a few hundred yards to visit the old 'sea front' before retracing.

PARKGATE

Situated on the edge of the Dee Estuary, this was once one of several anchorages where ships which were too large to reach Chester would unload their goods. It became a terminal for packet ships taking passengers to and from Dublin and, from 1760 until 1815, was also a seaside resort. The canalisation of the River Dee then changed the course of the river. The tide came in twice a day until about 1940 when the marsh spread rapidly. The area is now a bird reserve, visited by many thousands of migrant waders and wildfowl. The village is famous for its locally caught seafood and locally made ice cream.

THE WIRRAL WAY AND MILLENNIUM ROUTES 5 AND 56

The Wirral Country Park was created along the track of a railway line linking Chester to West Kirby which ceased to operate in 1963. There are attractive, maturely wooded, cuttings and embankments which provide vantage points with magnificent views over farmland and the Dee to the Welsh hills beyond. The Way has been incorporated into Millennium Routes 5 and 56 which follow quiet lanes and bridleways, the Shropshire Union Canal, and another disused railway, the Mickle Trafford to Dee Marsh line. This once carried steel through Chester to and from the steelworks on the banks of the Dee at Hawarden Bridge in Wales.

CHESTER CITY CENTRE

Chester is one of the most beautiful cities in Britain and has an important Roman, medieval and Tudor history and heritage, much of which is well preserved, including: a Roman amphitheatre, the only shrine to the goddess Minerva preserved in its original site, the only complete city walls in Britain, and the famous Rows, now shopping arcades, originally built in the 13th century. Tourist Information: 01244 402111.

NESS BOTANIC GARDENS

In 1898 Arthur Kilpin Bulley bought Mickwell Brow, a hill overlooking the Dee Estuary, and set about constructing his house and gardens which, from the first, were open to the public. Bulley's passion was exotic plants of the Himalayas and China and he sponsored the expeditions of George Forrest to collect their seeds. After Bulley's death in 1942, his daughter presented the collection to Liverpool University and, after modernisation, these have become one of the foremost botanic gardens in Britain. There is an admission fee. Information: 0151 353 0123. www.merseyworld.com/nessgardens

2

Delamere Forest and Manley Mere

15 or 28 miles

North-west Cheshire has a wide variety of scenery, whilst being easy cycling country. This ride starts in the Delamere Forest, now part of the 'Mersey Forest', which in Norman times was known as the Mara and Mondrum. The many meres in the area were formed from icebergs which were left behind by the retreating glaciers of the last Ice Age. The shorter ride (15 miles) visits a mere at Manley and returns via the unusually scattered village of Kelsall whilst the full route (28 miles) also takes in the marshes of the Mersey Estuary and Helsby Iron Age Hill Fort.

Map: OS Landranger 117 Chester & Wrexham (GR 543715).

Starting point: Barnsbridge Gates picnic area. *By car:* from the A556 west of Northwich, take the B5152 towards Frodsham and turn left at Hatchmere, the car park is eventually on the left. *By train:* start from Delamere Station. *By cycle:* from route 3 or the Cheshire Cycleway.

Refreshments: The Ring O'Bells in Frodsham, the Railway Inn in Helsby, the lakeside café at Manley Mere and Delamere Forest Visitor Centre café.

The routes: Both are almost entirely on lanes, the full route including just over 2 miles of broad, firmly surfaced forest trails, 3 miles of estuary byways and 2 miles of B road. The short route involves only the forest trails and a few hundred yards of B road. Whilst a high proportion of the terrain is flat, both routes have hilly sections which require low gears.

Turn L out of the picnic area, onto the lane, to ride through mature woodland. **Turn R** at the crossroads (signposted Manley, Frodsham). *For the short route, go straight on at the next junction and soon **turn L** to rejoin the long route at Sugar Lane.* Otherwise, **turn R** at the cross roads (Newpale Road – signposted Kingswood). There are fine views of rolling pasture and woodland to the right and glimpses over the Dee to the Welsh mountains to the left and, increasingly, views over the industrial Mersey Estuary ahead. **Turn R** at the next crossroads (signposted Frodsham). On the descent, **turn L** (Simon's Lane – signposted Forest Hills Hotel). Pass Frodsham golf course on the left, cross the Sandstone Way on Beacon Hill and, after the hotel, the road descends steeply to the outskirts of Frodsham.

Windsurfing instruction on Manley Mere, overlooked by the distant Helsby Hill

Turn **L** at the T-junction by the Ring O'Bells pub (Howey Lane) and descend (beware, speed bumps). Turn **R** at the T-junction opposite Netherton Hall and very soon **turn L** (unsignposted). Keep right at a fork, go under the railway, follow the road round a left-hand bend and in about 400 yards **turn R** onto an unsealed road (signposted as a footpath, though it is a right of way for vehicles) which leads over the motorway bridge. **Turn L** at the crossroads (unsignposted). There are views left, over the reclaimed marshes to Helsby Hill. **Turn L** before the chemical works (unsignposted) towards Helsby Hill. Turn **R** at the T-junction, then go through a farmyard and over the motorway and railway bridges to regain tarmac.

Go straight over the crossroads by the Railway Inn (Rake Lane – signposted 'one-way') and ascend the narrow lane between sandstone cliffs. **Turn R** at the T-junction (signposted 'one-way'). You may wish to park and scramble a few hundred yards on one of three footpaths which lead left from this lane, through National Trust woodland, to the Iron Age hill fort near the summit of Helsby Hill.

Continue, to **turn R** at a T-junction (signposted Tarvin) and go through

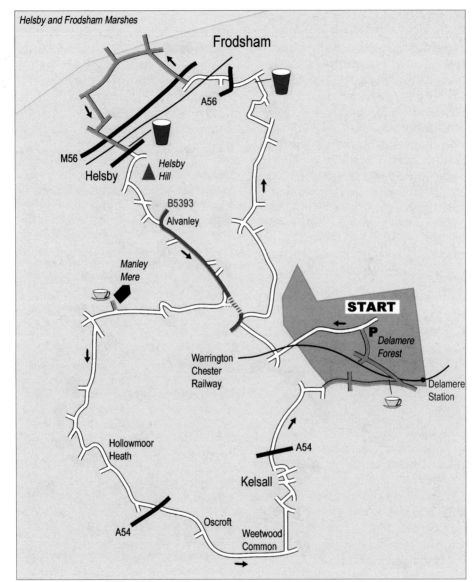

Alvanley village. Ascend a 13% hill, past a Manley parish sign and **turn R** (School Lane – signed 'School'). **Turn R** at a T-junction (Sugar Lane). *The short route joins here.*

As you approach a hairpin bend,

Manley Mere can be glimpsed ahead, in the distance, through the trees. Descend and eventually **turn R** to Manley Mere with its lakeside café (signposted Windsurfing Centre).

15

Retrace to the road and **turn R** to continue. **Turn L** (signposted Cheshire Cycleway) and take the **second turn L** (Barnhouse Lane, eventually signposted Great Barrow). Soon after entering a sandstone cutting on a rise, **turn L** (unsignposted, eventually signed Irons Lane, becomes Hollowmoor Heath). **Turn L** at a T-junction (signposted Tarvin). **Turn L** (signposted Oscroft). Go straight over the crossroads at the A54 (Shay Lane – signposted Oscroft). Continue through Oscroft and the road is signed to Willington. Take the next **turn L** (signposted Kelsall).

On the outskirts of Kelsall take the **second turn L** (Church Street), go over the crossroads (Church Street North), **turn R** at the T-junction (Old Coach Road), immediately **turn L** (signed 'one-way'), **turn L** at the T-junction in front of the Methodist church and follow the lane closest to the church. **Turn R** at the T-junction (unsignposted) to go under a major road and ride alongside woodland. **Turn R** on a left-hand bend (unsignposted) onto a single track lane. **Turn L** on a right-hand bend onto an unsealed road (signposted Linmere). Go straight on past the barrier at Grey's Gate. Continue over the crossroads passing Eddisbury Lodge entrance on the left. After speed bumps **turn L** into Delamere Forest Visitor Centre.

Turn L out of the centre and immediately **turn L** over a sandstone bridge (waymarked blue cycle route). **Turn R** at a crossroads (waymarked blue cycle route, Hunger Hill Trail). **Turn R** at a T-junction with a road and immediately **turn R** into Barnsbridge Gates picnic area.

• •

DELAMERE FOREST

In Norman times, this forest stretched from Nantwich in the south to the banks of the River Mersey in the north and the kings claimed it for private hunting, fencing it to protect the royal deer. Some areas were drained in Napoleonic times and planted for commercial forestry; however, the Forestry Commission, current trustees of the forest, have now re-flooded Blakemere Moss to create a boggy wildlife sanctuary which is a haven for the beautiful small tortoiseshell butterfly, greater spotted woodpecker, white faced darter dragonfly, green woodpecker, siskin and southern hawker dragonfly. There are two waymarked cycle routes in the forest which are easy riding: the blue route (4 miles) and the white route (7 miles). More are envisaged, so it is worthwhile calling at the visitor centre for the latest information. Telephone 01606 889792.

FRODSHAM AND HELSBY

There were Stone Age and Iron Age settlements on the hills of the area and traces remain today at Helsby but the first known settlers in Frodsham were Anglo-Saxons of the kingdom of Mercia. Helsby was settled by the Vikings who, in the 10th century AD, moved into the Wirral as far as Helsby or Hjallr-by (the village on the ledge). The Frodsham population, about 1,250 in 1801, grew after the railway arrived in 1850 but, whilst

En route to Delamere Forest Visitor Centre

modern industries flourish to the north and west, Frodsham and Helsby have retained much of their rural character.

KELSALL

This unusual village owes its origin to the break in the sandstone ridge which forms a barrier across Cheshire from Frodsham to Tarporley. In prehistoric times the route was protected by the Iron Age forts on Eddisbury Hill and Kelsborrow Hill and the Romans later brought Watling Street through the gap, a vital road which carried salt from mid-Cheshire to pay the garrison at Chester their 'salarium'. A combination of work in the local quarries and forest, the road, and fresh water, led to a hamlet being born, but even in late medieval times there was no church, village green or manor house to provide a centre, so the township straggled along the road, hemmed in on both sides by the forest.

Delamere Forest, Little Budworth and the Whitegate Way

19 miles

This ride explores more of the ancient forest of Mara and Mondrum (see also route 2) and its associated lowland meres in north-west Cheshire. Starting again from Delamere Forest, we set off south-east to visit Little Budworth Common and utilise the Whitegate Way to view Abbot's Moss and Newchurch Common, passing on the way the race circuit of Oulton Park with its tragic history.

Maps: OS Landranger 117 Chester & Wrexham and 118 Stoke-on-Trent & Macclesfield (GR 543715).

Starting point: Barnsbridge Gates picnic area. *By car:* from the A556 west of Northwich, take the B5152 towards Frodsham and turn left at Hatchmere; the car park is eventually on the left. *By train:* start from Delamere Station. *By cycle:* from route 2.

Refreshments: The Delamere Forest Visitor Centre café, Summertrees Tea Room on the Sandstone Trail, the Coffee Shop at Cotebrook, the Red Lion pub in Little Budworth and the Tiger's Head in Norley.

The route: Quiet lanes with approximately 2 miles of forest roads, 1½ miles of the Whitegate Way and just under ½ mile of bridleway.

Turn L out of the car park and immediately **turn L** onto an unsealed forest road which climbs for a few yards and then levels off and broadens. Follow the blue cycle route waymarks through the forest (see ride 4), keeping right as a minor trail goes left. **Turn L** at the crossroads onto an equally broad unsealed road and again keep right as minor trails go left. Cross a sandstone bridge and immediately **turn R**, passing the Delamere Visitor Centre on the right. Go over the crossroads, passing Eddisbury Lodge on the right. Continue straight on at the barrier and eventually **turn L** at the T-junction onto tarmac (Yeld Lane).

Climb over the hill, passing The Yeld, a local common, on the left. Cross the A54 on a bridge and soon go straight over a crossroads by Th'ouse at Top pub (Waste Lane). **Turn L** at a T-junction (unsignposted) onto a fine ridge road with distant views over the Peckforton Hills to the right and Delamere Forest to the left. Pass Summertrees Tea Room, alongside the Sandstone Trail, on the left, and eventually Tirley Garth, 'A Quiet Garden', (admission fee) on the right. Pass one turn to Utkinton on the right and Primrose Wood on the left and take the next **turn R** (Quarry Bank – signposted Utkinton). Take the first **turn L** (unsignposted) for a long descent with views ahead to the distant Peak District hills.

Turn R at a T-junction (unsignposted, eventually signed Hollins Hill). **Turn L** at a T-junction (unsignposted) and very soon go straight over a crossroads, passing a church on the right. Soon after go straight over the crossroads by the Coffee Shop café (Oulton Mill Lane). **Turn L** (signposted Leisure Drive) and soon **turn L** at a T-junction (unsignposted) to pass the Mill Pool Restaurant on the left and ride over the dam of the lovely pool.

As the lane enters woodland, tempting paths lead off to the left into Little Budworth Common Country Park. Pass the entrance to Oulton Park on the right (you may have been aware of a distant squealing of tyres). Entering Little Budworth note Dodd's House, an attractive brick and sandstone almshouse, dated 1734, on the left. Pass the Red Lion on the right, St

Peter's church on the left and, leaving the village, Little Budworth Mere. **Turn R** at a crossroads (Park Road – signposted Whitegate) and soon go over another crossroads (Clay Lane – signposted Whitegate Way).

Immediately before a narrow bridge with traffic lights, **turn R** (signposted Whitegate Way) to Whitegate Station and **turn L** onto the Whitegate Way, passing under the bridge. The surface is firm stone and earth and there are fine views, at first over pastureland and then over a series of meres and wooded wetlands with Newchurch Common to the right and Abbot's Moss and Nunsmere to the left. **Turn L** in front of a brick bridge over the trail and **turn R** to cross the bridge on a sandy bridleway which is soon firm stone. Pass the Scouts' Forest Camp on the right, go through a barrier and over a crossroads (unsignposted). There is a short stretch of stony bridleway and then a narrow tarmac lane, eventually signed Kennel Lane.

Go straight over the crossroads (Weaverham Road). **Turn L** at the crossroads (Norley Road – signposted Cuddington). Go straight over the crossroads at the traffic lights (signposted Norley) and immediately **turn R** (Mill Lane). **Turn L** at a T-junction (Cuddington Lane) and soon **turn R** (unsignposted, eventually signed Barrastich Lane). **Turn L** at a T-junction (unsignposted, soon

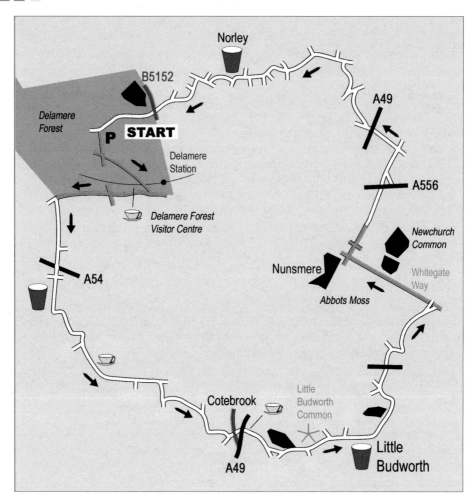

signed Cheshire Cycleway). In Norley, pass the Tiger's Head pub on the right, and soon **turn R** (Maddock's Hill – signposted Kingsley, Cheshire Cycleway). **Turn R** at a T-junction (signposted Cheshire Cycleway) noting the quotes on the wall of the Temperance Hall opposite. **Turn L** (Post Office Lane – signposted Cheshire Cycleway). Continue straight over the crossroads by the

Zion Chapel (signposted Cheshire Cycleway), through the forest and eventually **turn L** into Barnsbridge Gates picnic area.

• • • • • • • • • • • • • • • • • • •

LITTLE BUDWORTH COUNTRY PARK

A remnant of the ancient hunting forest of Mara and Mondrum, this is a splendid example of lowland heathland. It is home to green woodpeckers and, in summer, tree pipits, wood warblers and willow

Cycle hire at the Delamere Visitor Centre

warblers. There is a pond and a Heathland Trail, whose areas of purple heather are gradually being extended.

LITTLE BUDWORTH, ST PETER'S CHURCH AND OULTON PARK

The village is named in Domesday Book and a church existed before 1190. The tower of St Peter's church was built between 1490 and 1526 and was formerly used as a beacon. The church interior has been restored and of the early fittings only the Georgian pulpit and a 17th century font survive. On the south side is a memorial window to twin brothers killed in action in the Great War, Philip de Malpas Egerton and Rowland Le Belward Egerton, the sons of the local landowning family of Oulton Park. The Egertons' house at Oulton Park was partly destroyed by fire in the 1926 and demolished by enemy bombs in 1940. The park became the Oulton Park motor racing track, the North of England's most important venue.

WHITEGATE WAY

The Whitegate railway line carried salt, for almost 100 years, from the mines along the west bank of the River Weaver to Cuddington, where it joined the Chester-Manchester line. This line finally closed in 1966 and today, in combination with the Weaver Cycleway, provides a traffic-free link from Winsford to Cuddington.

Lymm, Great Budworth and the Anderton Boat Lift

33 miles

This ride, commencing on a flat section of the Trans Pennine Trail, visits some lovingly restored relics of our rural and industrial past. Taking to lanes, west of Altrincham, the route passes Dunham Massey Deer Park and the grounds of Arley Hall to visit Great Budworth, a village whose old world charm was celebrated in the *Hinge and Bracket* television series. Continuing, through Marbury Country Park on roads closed to motor traffic and cycle paths, we visit the massive boat lift, now restored to working order, before returning on lanes to the Trail.

Maps: OS Landranger 109 Manchester and 118 Stoke-on-Trent & Macclesfield (GR 678876).

Starting point: Statham Avenue Trans Pennine Trail car park, Lymm. *By car:* from the A56 in Lymm, follow signs first to the village centre and then to the Lymm Hotel in Statham Avenue. The car park is opposite the hotel. *By train:* the nearest station to the route is Hale, 1½ miles from Dunham Park. *By cycle:* from route 5 or the towns of Warrington and Altrincham via the Trail.

Refreshments: The Swan with Two Nicks in Little Bollington, the George and Dragon in Budworth, the Thorn Inn in Appleton Thorn, or the Parr Arms in Grappenhall.

The route: Flat and gently rolling lanes with a total of 6 miles of smooth unsealed trails and less than a mile of B roads.

Turn **R** onto the Trail which leads through attractive suburbs into open country. Cross a series of level crossings and pass the Railway Inn. Then leave the Trail at the second level crossing, characterised by ornate, heavy, black metal fixtures. Turn **R** onto the lane (Station Road) and very soon, opposite the Rope and Anchor pub, **turn L** (Back Lane). Go over the Bridgewater Canal and **turn R** at the T-junction (School Lane becomes Woodhouse Lane – signposted Altrincham). **Turn R** at the T-junction (Woodhouse Lane). Pass the entrance to Dunham Massey Park and immediately **turn L** (signposted Footpath, Bollington Mill). This little tarmac lane is a public footpath so you should walk, soon with views to the left

Taking a rest in Little Bollington

over Dunham Massey Hall and Park, as far as the River Bollin and over the narrow footbridge.

Remount and follow the lane ahead to pass the Swan with Two Nicks pub. Keep left on the winding lane and **turn L** at the T-junction by the Stamford Arms and immediately **turn R** (Reddy Lane – signposted Millington). Go under the motorway (note the plaque commemorating the preaching of John Wesley) and the lane becomes Booth Bank Lane. **Turn L** (Thowler Lane becomes Back Lane – signposted High Legh). **Turn R** at the T-junction (Peacock Lane – signposted High Legh). First **turn L** (Broadoak Lane), noting the huge hollow trunk held together by an iron band, at the corner. **Turn R** at the T-junction, passing the local golf course, and **turn L** immediately after the 30 mph signs (Pheasant Walk), to climb gently through High Legh with its ancient sandstone chapel on the left. **Turn L** at the T-junction (unsignposted) and soon **turn L** (signposted Knutsford, A50) and immediately **turn L** and **turn R** over the A50 (Halliwells Brow – signposted Great Budworth).

After passing over the motorway, look for the second bridleway on the right to view a rhyming

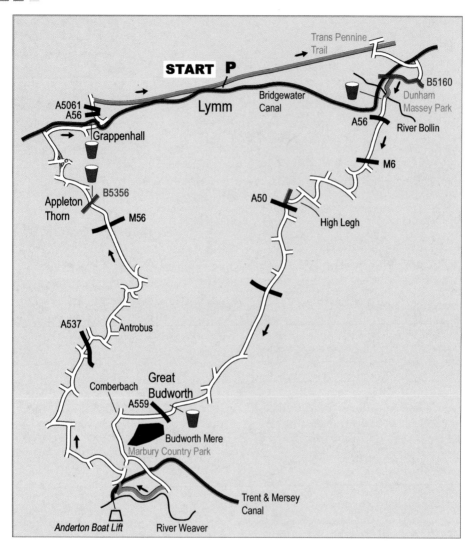

signpost, one of several accredited to Rowland Egerton Warburton of Arley. Continue and **turn R** at the T-junction (signposted Great Budworth). Take the second through road **turning R** (Westgate Lane – signposted Great Budworth) to visit delightful Great Budworth where there are more examples of

Warburton's verse, notably on the front porch of the George and Dragon pub.

Continue over the crossroads (Budworth Lane – signposted Comberbach) and climb for views to the left over Budworth Mere and Northwich. **Turn L** at the crossroads in Comberbach (Warrington Road – signposted Northwich) and after about ¾ mile **turn L** (signposted Marbury Country Park). Continue straight on past the 'no motor vehicles' sign, over the canal, and straight on through the bridleway gate. Soon **turn R** (signposted Cheshire County Council, Anderton Boat Lift and Nature Park) through a chicane onto a smooth unsealed path. Almost immediately **turn L**.

Follow the paths by the river: **turn L** at waymark number 6 when the main path leaves the river, **turn L** onto the minor river path opposite the chemical works and soon, around the bend ahead, the massive, boat lift can be seen. Through the chicane **turn L** to visit the exhibition centre and view the lift at close quarters.

To exit, retrace to the chicane, then follow the car park signs up the hill. Exit the car park over the canal bridge and **turn R** (unsignposted). Soon **turn L** (Cogshall Lane becomes Hough Lane). **Turn R** at the T-junction (unsignposted). **Turn L** at the T-junction (signposted Runcorn) soon passing a Little Leigh village sign. **Turn R** (Hall Lane – signposted Antrobus) soon passing an Antrobus village sign. **Turn L** at the T-junction (signposted Whitley). Take the second **turn R** (Wheatsheaf Lane – signposted Stretton) and go straight over the crossroads at the Antrobus Arms

The Anderton boat lift

(unsignposted). **Turn R** at the T-junction (Knutsford Road) and soon **turn L** in Antrobus village (Barbers Lane – signposted Arley).

Turn L at the crossroads (New Road – signposted Appleton). Continue over the motorway to Appleton Thorn where you go over the crossroads by the Thorn Inn. **Turn L** before the roundabout signposted Warrington, immediately after the 30 mph sign (signposted as a 'no through road'), straight on over the main road on the cycle crossing and **turn R** at the end of the cycle path (signposted 'Grappenhall' from the main road). Before the traffic lights at the aqueduct, **turn R** (Stockton Lane). **Turn R** at the T-junction and soon **turn L** (Church Lane) into Grappenhall.

Go past the church, over the canal, and **turn L** (Glebe Avenue). **Turn R** at the T-junction (Lindi Avenue). Go over the crossroads (East View) and the next crossroads (Bradshaw Lane) to soon pass under a bridge and immediately **turn R** through a chicane (signposted Trans Pennine Trail). Follow the Trail, passing under the motorway, to Statham Avenue car park.

LYMM

Lymm grew rapidly after the completion of the Bridgewater Canal in the 1770s and again when the London and North Western Railway was opened in 1853. In the last century, this line was considered uneconomic and the disused track has now been rejuvenated as part of the Trans Pennine Trail.

THE TRANS PENNINE TRAIL (NATIONAL CYCLE ROUTE 62)

This purpose-built route crosses northern England from the Mersey to the Humber. Mostly off-road, the Trail uses existing rights of way, riverbank paths, canal towpaths and disused railway lines through widely contrasting landscape, from rural areas to cities where former industrial sites have been reclaimed as woodlands and nature reserves.

DUNHAM MASSEY DEER PARK

Entrance to the 250 acres of medieval deer park, ancient woodland, ponds and pasture is free to cyclists (who must wheel their bikes) and walkers. The estate is in the care of the National Trust along with the 18th century moated mansion, formal gardens and Dunham Massey Mill. There is an admission charge to the house and gardens. Information: 0161 941 1025. www.nationaltrust.org.uk

GREAT BUDWORTH

This is a typical old Cheshire village of black and white cottages, each with its own character. St Mary's parish church dates from the 14th century and inside are five 13th century oak stalls which could be the oldest in Cheshire. Outside, set in the church wall, are the village stocks which were in use up to 1854.

MARBURY COUNTRY PARK

This consists of 200 acres of prime habitat ranging from a deep mere to deciduous woodland and open grassland. The park was a country estate but now the Cheshire Countryside Management Service runs the area as a country park open to all. Cormorants and rare migrating birds are often seen in winter and the reed beds have been home to several bittern over the last few years.

THE ANDERTON BOAT LIFT

Built in 1875, this is an elegant example of the Victorians' mastery of cast iron and hydraulics. It satisfied the need for heavy commercial and industrial canal traffic to navigate between the River Weaver and the Trent & Mersey Canal by providing a more efficient means of transferring goods than the labour intensive inclined planes, hoists and chutes. It has been restored to working order by the Anderton Boat Lift Trust.

GRAPPENHALL

A picturesque village complete with cobblestones, village stocks and ancient Norman church, St Wilfrid's, with a Saxon font. It is said that a stone carving on the church tower may be the original Cheshire Cat and the inspiration for the grinning cat in Lewis Carroll's book *Alice's Adventures in Wonderland*.

Arley, Tatton Deer Park, Knutsford and Great Budworth

28 miles

This undemanding ride in some of Cheshire's flattest lanes visits two lovely parks: Arley Hall, still in private hands but with a bridleway through the grounds, and Tatton Park, a vast, picturesque National Trust estate which offers an off-road, though tarmac, route into Knutsford. On your way round there is the opportunity to visit the Penny Farthing Museum which is housed in a Knutsford café, to picnic at the remote birthplace of Lewis Carroll near Daresbury, and to view Rostherne Mere, the largest lake in Cheshire.

Maps: OS Landranger 109 Manchester and 118 Stoke on Trent & Macclesfield (GR 670810).

Starting point: The walkers' car park, Arley. *By car:* from the M6 junction 20, take the A50/B5356 to Appleton Thorne where turn left to Arley village. The small car park is on the left. *By train:* from Knutsford Station, joining the route in King Street. *By cycle:* from route 4.

Refreshments: There is a restaurant in Tatton Park, the Courtyard Coffee House and Museum in Knutsford and, a few hundred yards off the route, the Dones Green transport café is popular with cyclists. The pubs mentioned en route also serve food.

The route: Flat lanes and tarmac rights of way with about ¼ mile of bumpy, beaten earth bridleway and a few hundred yards of urban streets.

Turn L out of the car park, through the stone gateway into the Arley estate (signposted 'private, bridleway') and very soon **turn L**, as indicated by the rhyming wooden signpost, onto a road designated as a bridleway. Eventually, after a short stretch of cobbles, **turn L** (signposted as a bridle and cycle way) through a gate to follow a beaten earth path which runs in a straight line, at first at the field's edge alongside woodland, and then across the field to a metal bridleway gate into woodland. Very soon **turn R** (Conn Lane – signposted as a bridleway) and soon **turn R** onto tarmac and cobbles and over a stream bridge. **Turn L** at the T-junction in front of the attractive brick and timber-frame Mill House.

Turn L at the T-junction onto

Tatton Deer Park

public roads (unsignposted). Go over the motorway and take the first **turn R** (signposted Hoo Green). Straight over the crossroads by the Kilton pub and restaurant (unsignposted). **Turn L** at the T-junction onto the A556 (or use the pavement); immediately **turn R** at the traffic lights (Mereside Road – signposted Tatton Park) and immediately **turn L** (signposted Rostherne). The lane winds through woodland and past Cicely Mill pool to attractive Rostherne village (note the pump on the right at the junction). Here our way lies right but, to view the church and mere, **turn L** at the T-junction (unsignposted) and very soon **turn R** to the churchyard. Rostherne Mere can be viewed from the north side of the church. Retrace your route to the village pump and continue.

Go over the crossroads (signposted Tatton Park Entrance), noting the time that the gates close (usually 7 pm). Follow the signposts, **turning L** (signposted Parkland, Knutsford), through magnificent parkland, looking out for deer and passing Tatton Mere. Exit through the stone gateway and almost immediately **turn L** onto a path as the road bends right. When the path ends, continue ahead, on foot, along King Street (one-way),

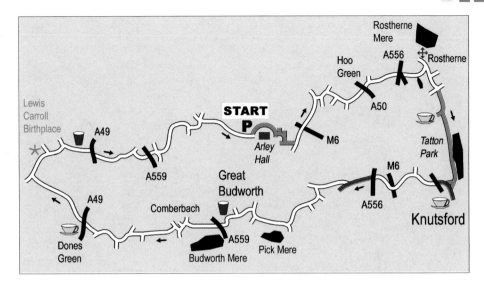

soon passing the Angel Inn and White Lion on the right, and immediately **turn R** through a small gateway into a courtyard to visit the Penny Farthing Museum on the left.

Retrace your route, **turning L** outside the courtyard onto King Street, which becomes Garden Road, passing the Tatton Park entrance on the right. Continue over the crossroads (Tabley Road), passing The Heath, a Site of Special Scientific Interest with heathland and reed beds, on the left, and soon out into open country. Go over the motorway bridge and eventually over the crossroads at the Windmill pub (signposted Pickmere, B5391).

Turn R (Budworth Road – signposted Arley Hall) and eventually, after a small wood, take the first **turn L** (Frog Lane). **Turn R**

at the T-junction (Park Lane), soon with views over Pick Mere to the left. After a red, traditional phone box and thatched house, **turn L** (Westage Lane – signposted Great Budworth) to pass through picturesque Great Budworth. Go over the crossroads (Budworth Lane – signposted Comberbach), soon with views over Budworth Mere to the left, and into Comberbach. Here **turn L** at the T-junction (Warrington Lane – signposted Northwich); soon take the second **turn R** (Senna Lane – signposted Whitley) and soon **turn L** (Cogshall Lane – signposted Dones Green). Past the Little Leigh parish sign the road becomes Ash House Lane then, after Little Leigh Baptist church, pass a 'no through road' on the right and take the next **turn R** (Heath Lane).

At the crossroads, the transport café is a few hundred yards to the left,

Knutsford Penny Farthing Museum

on the right hand side. Otherwise, continue over the crossroads (Marsh Lane). **Turn R** at the T-junction opposite Thatched House Farm (unsignposted). Soon note the entrance to the newly planted Lewis Carroll Centenary Wood on the left and then soon **turn L** (Morphany Lane) and immediately **turn L** through a bridleway gate and take the path to visit the site of Lewis Carroll's early home.

Retrace your route and **turn R** outside the gate, then immediately **turn L** at the T-junction (signposted 'Borough of Halton', eventually signed for Norcott Brook, Higher Green Lane and Grimsditch Lane). Pass the Millstone pub on the left and the old mill pool. **Turn R** at the T-junction (Tarporley Road) and immediately **turn L** (Raddel Lane – signposted Higher Whitley). The road passes some small meres, popular for fishing, a lovely duck pond on the outskirts of Whitley, and becomes Bentleys Farm Lane. **Turn R** (Lake Lane – signposted Arley), passing more fishing waters. Go over the crossroads (Knutsford Road) and on the first bend **turn L** (Reed Lane – signposted Whitley Reed).

Turn L at the T-junction (signposted Arley). **Turn R** at the crossroads (unsignposted, eventually signed to Arley Hall, 'no through road'). Soon **turn L** into the walkers' car park.

• •

ARLEY

Arley Hall, with over 100 acres of gardens and parkland, has been owned and run by the same family for more than 500 years. The original hall was built by Piers Warburton in 1486 and the cruck barn and other outbuildings date from that period. There are admission charges to the house and gardens. Information: 01565 777353.

ROSTHERNE CHURCH AND MERE

St Mary's church at Rostherne is famous for its beautiful setting. Some of the stonework inside the building is of the Early English style from around 1200 but the church is the work of many different periods and the tower was rebuilt in 1742–4. Rostherne Mere, covering 119 acres, is a National Nature Reserve renowned for its bird life but there is no public access and the best view is from the churchyard. It is said that centuries ago one of the church bells came away from its ropes and rolled into the mere and, after this had happened three times, the local workmen left it there. At dawn on Easter Day a mermaid swims into the mere through a channel from the Irish Sea and rings the bell.

TATTON PARK

This is one of the most complete estates open to visitors. Its two historic houses are set in 1,000 acres of beautiful rolling parkland with lakes, tree-lined avenues and woodland which offer a wonderful setting for cycling, walking, sailing, fishing, enjoying picnics or watching the herds of red and fallow deer and other wildlife. Access to the parkland is free for cyclists and walkers. For an admission fee, you can visit the richly decorated neo-classical mansion which houses magnificent collections of furniture, glassware, porcelain and fine art. In 1982 this was used in several scenes for the TV serial *Brideshead Revisited*. Tatton's 50 acres of pleasure grounds include a terraced Italian garden, the palatial glass fernery, and the famous Japanese garden. There is also a working farm with rare breeds. Information: 01625 534400. www.tattonpark.org.uk

BIRTHPLACE OF LEWIS CARROLL

Now an attractively maintained picnic spot, the parsonage where Charles Lutwidge Dodgson, Lewis Carroll, the author of *Alice in Wonderland*, was brought up as the eldest son of eleven children was so remotely situated in the middle of open fields, that a passing farm cart was an 'event' for these children. Charles helped out with running the household by entertaining his brothers and sisters and perhaps it was from this activity that he developed his love of entertaining children. There is a plan of the parsonage on the site of the building, and a plaque showing details of the Dodgson family.

Marple, the Middlewood Way and Lyme Park

16 miles

This route skirts the foothills of the Peak District in north-east Cheshire. The views are splendid and much of the ride is off-road since we utilise some of our legacy from the area's rich history. Commencing on the Middlewood Way, a wooded linear park through gentle pastureland, we proceed to Lyme Park, a National Trust property comprising 1,400 acres of open moorland and landscaped 18th century parkland, the setting for the BBC production of *Pride and Prejudice*, and then return over Marple Ridge with spectacular views simultaneously east and west.

Maps: OS Landranger 109 Manchester and 118 Stoke-on-Trent & Macclesfield (GR 950887).

Starting point: Marple Rose Hill Station car park. *By car:* from the A626 Stockport/Marple road. Rose Hill Station and the Middlewood Way are signed on the western Marple outskirts. *By train:* the Marple Rose Hill service from Manchester Piccadilly. *By cycle:* from routes 7 and 8.

Refreshments: Look for signs on the Middlewood Way to the Boar's Head and Coffee Tavern at the site of Poynton Station, and the Miner's Arms and Lyme View Café at Wood Lane. In Bollington the Dog and Partridge offers bar snacks. There is a second Coffee Tavern on Shrigley Road. Lyme Park has a café and restaurant.

The route: Approximately 7 miles of flat, unsealed tracks and 9 miles of gently rolling tarmac roads with three short steep climbs.

From Rose Hill Station car park **turn L** (signposted Middlewood Way) and immediately **turn L** again, past a carved wooden fox, onto a narrow path which within yards opens out into a broad woodland track though a shallow cutting. In winter this can be muddy but I have never found it unridable.

As the surrounding countryside falls away, views of the Cheshire Plain and Pennine foothills can be glimpsed and the Way's firm crushed stone base is revealed. Through a tunnel under the busy A6, the path enters another wooded cutting as far as Middlewood Station where, after crossing the Manchester/Buxton

Riders on Poynton station platform, part of the Middlewod Way

railway line on a viaduct, we are offered a choice of two paths. I tend to use the walkers' and cyclists' path in winter and the broader horse riders' path in summer.

From the walkers' path, the adjacent Jackson's Brickyard nature area is signed. This has been designated a Site of Biological Importance as the old clay pits hold ponds where great crested newts breed. At the site of Poynton Station, the original track becomes a picnic area whilst the Way takes to the platform, from where refreshments and the Nelson Pit Visitor Centre are signed.

Approaching Bollington viaduct, dismount and walk down the steep path left, down the side of the viaduct. There are views ahead of White Nancy (see ride 7). Go past the skateboard ramps on the left, and a Ranger's office and toilets on the right, to emerge, **turning R**, (no signpost). **Turn L** at the T-junction (Wellington Road becomes Palmerston Street), go past the Dog and Partridge, under the aqueduct, through the traffic lights and, immediately after a little church on the left, either engage bottom gear or dismount to **turn sharp L** (Beeston Brow). As the road levels it becomes Long Lane.

Turn L at a T-junction (unsigned) and soon **turn R** (Shrigley Road – signposted Higher Poynton). The route now follows the boundary of the Peak District National Park. On

33

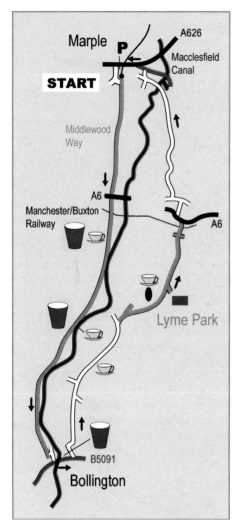

Parkgate. *If it is evening and Lyme Park is shut, retrace to the chapel and continue the descent to rejoin the Middlewood Way, at the little car park on the left, back to Marple.*

A wooden bridleway gate leads into Lyme Park and an idyllic climb through woodland, alongside a stream, on a well-beaten unsurfaced road. The trees slowly give way to rhododendrons and finally bracken. At the top, another gate leads onto tarmac through open parkland, a favourite place for kite flying at weekends and sledging in winter.

As the road dips towards the mill pond, with its tea room, watch out for pedestrians but if the way is clear it is possible to attain enough speed to surmount the next rise. Here a T-junction offers Lyme Hall and Lyme Park restaurant to the right. **Turn L** for a long descent straight over the crossroads at the toll kiosk and over a cattle grid and railway bridge, and out through the main gates to a T-junction at the busy A6 (families might like to remain on the pavement for 20 yards to the left here). **Turn L** and immediately **turn R** (Light Alders Lane) and ascend. **Turn L** at the T-junction (no signpost) and soon **turn R** (Wybersley Road) onto a narrow, rolling, winding lane with one steep little climb past the Romper pub and then magnificent views from Marple Ridge, simultaneously over the Cheshire Plain to the left and the Derbyshire

the right, as the road climbs gently, is a Coffee Tavern. When the lane starts a serious descent, signed 11%, watch for a small chapel on the right. Here, as the road bends left, a narrow tarmac lane leads ahead. **Turn R** down this lane (unsigned). At the bottom of the dip, over a little stream, **turn R** in front of the gatehouse at West

hills to the right. Descending into Marple the road becomes first Ridge Road and then Church Lane. Look right at the canal bridge after the Ring O'Bells pub to see colourful Marple boatyard and the junction of the Macclesfield and Peak Forest Canals, surmounted by its snake bridge.

Take the third exit at the mini-roundabout and **turn L** at the T-junction (traffic lights, Stockport Road) and go straight through the next traffic lights and, before long, over the railway to Rose Hill Station on the left.

• •

MARPLE

Marple's attraction lies in its situation, between the Peak District and the Cheshire Plain. The Peak Forest Canal, which extends northwards into Greater Manchester and south to Whaley Bridge, with an arm to Buxworth, is an important leisure facility, having a junction in Marple with the Macclesfield Canal, part of the Cheshire Ring.

MIDDLEWOOD WAY

The Middlewood Way was originally the Macclesfield, Bollington and Marple railway line, built in the 1860s, closed for goods and passenger traffic in 1970, and opened as a path for walkers, cyclists and horse riders in 1985. The 11 mile way, part of National Cycle Route 55, has been planted with trees and shrubs, now mature, and is a wildlife refuge.

Lyme Park

LYME PARK

The parkland is grazed by herds of red and fallow deer and overlooked by The Cage, a recently restored hunting lodge. The splendid mansion, which was built on the site of a medieval hall in the 1730s, has early 19th century additions, and houses collections of historic furniture, tapestries and clocks. The grounds are open daily and entrance is free to cyclists and walkers. There is a fee to visit the house and garden, which are open in summer.

Circuit of Macclesfield: Gawsworth Hall and Henbury

23 miles

This route starts in the Pennine foothills but soon descends to the Cheshire Plain, via Fool's Nook pub, to view rolling parkland and splendid halls dating from the 11th to the 20th century. Near Warren, we visit the late 15th century Gawsworth Hall, whose gardens were the location for the TV production of Sherlock Holmes's *Boscombe Valley Mystery*. Travelling northwards, we encounter the strange, modern Italian-style Henbury Hall, with its famous bluebell woods, and finally Adlington Hall, built on the site of an 11th century hunting lodge, the oak trees supports of which still form part of the building.

Maps: OS Landranger 118 Stoke-on-Trent & Macclesfield and 109 Manchester (GR 931781).

Starting point: Adlington Road car park, Bollington (note the evening closing time displayed). *By car:* from the A523 Stockport/Macclesfield road, turn east just north of Macclesfield, signposted Bollington. *By train:* Prestbury Station, 2 miles west of Bollington. *By cycle:* links to routes 6, 8, 9 and 10.

Refreshments: AJ's at Flora Tea Room in Henbury. Pubs serving snacks and meals include the Dog and Partridge in Bollington, the Redway Tavern at Kerridge, Fool's Nook, the Blacksmith's Arms at Henbury and the Legh Arms at Adlington.

The route: 23 miles of lanes, of which approximately 5 miles have steep ascents and descents requiring low gears and good brakes, whilst the remainder are gently rolling. A few hundred yards of A and B roads.

Turn **R** out of the car park and turn **L** at the T-junction (Palmerston Street), past the Dog and Partridge, and almost immediately **turn R** (signposted Cheshire Cycleway) to ascend over the Macclesfield Canal. **Turn L** at the T-junction (signposted Cheshire Cycleway, soon signed Jackson Lane) and at the top of the hill, just after the Bulls Head pub, **turn L** (Redway – signposted Cheshire Cycleway) and pass the Redway Tavern, noting the old inn sign and poem on the wall.

The road becomes Windmill Lane and climbs steeply with

Gawsworth Hall from the lake

magnificent views, first over Bollington and later over Macclesfield and the Cheshire Plain. Soon after the lane becomes Kerridge Road, **turn L** (Lidgetts Lane) to climb out of the woodland into open pasture and heathland bordered by dry gritstone walls.

Turn R at the T-junction, leaving the cycleway, and very soon **turn L** (Calrofold Lane). **Turn L** at the T-junction and soon **turn R** (both unsignposted). Then over the crossroads (Back Eddisbury Road). **Turn L** at the crossroads (unsignposted) and immediately **turn R** (Broadcar Road), which eventually becomes a narrow,

steep, winding descent to Langley. Here **turn R** at the T-junction (unsignposted).

Descend and **turn L** immediately after the Church House pub (signposted Cheshire Cycleway). Go over the crossroads (Walker Lane – signposted Lyme Green), noting the attractive Sutton Lane Ends village sign which commemorates the work of local wildlife artist Charles Tunnicliffe. First **turn L** (Parvey Lane – signposted Cheshire Cycleway) and **turn L** at the T-junction (signposted Cheshire Cycleway), soon passing Sutton Reservoir and climbing over a final low spur of

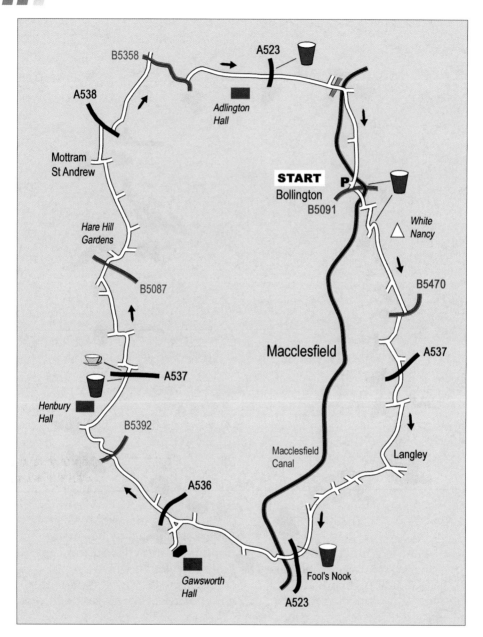

the Pennine foothills to Fool's Nook pub.

Cross the A523 and the metal

swing bridge over the Macclesfield Canal. Here we take the lane ahead (signposted Gawsworth) to Warren. Entering the village, just past the

The attractive village sign in Sutton Lane Ends

30 mph sign, **turn L** (Wardle Crescent) and **turn L** at the crossroads (Church Lane – signposted Congleton) to view Old Gawsworth Hall, a magnificent building in a splendid setting, best seen from the road across the lake by the church.

Retrace on Church Lane and continue straight on, past Maggoty's Grave on the left (see ride 9), into Warren village to cross over the A536 (Dark Lane – signposted Siddington). **Turn R** at the T-junction (signposted Macclesfield, B5392) and **immediately turn L** (Bearhurst Lane – signposted Chelford) noting the Victorian postbox in the house wall on the left. Soon the lane descends gently, with views over parkland ahead and to the right of

the surreal Henbury Hall, and then dips through the renowned bluebell woods to a T-junction at the hall gates. Here **turn R** (signposted Henbury), keeping an eye open for closer views of Henbury Hall to the left.

At the Blacksmith's Arms (with the Flora Garden Centre and Tea Rooms opposite), cross the A537 (Pepper Street – signposted Whirley) and **turn L** at the T-junction (unsignposted). **Turn L** at the next T-junction (Wrigley Lane – signposted Over Alderley) and first **turn R** (signposted Over Alderley). **Turn R** at the next T-junction (unsignposted), past Over Alderley Methodist church, to the Black Greyhound Smithy, where you **turn R** and **turn L** over the staggered crossroads onto a narrow lane (signposted Prestbury, Mottram St Andrew) to a T-junction.

Hare Hill Estate is ahead and there are National Trust gardens open in summer; an entrance is signposted a few hundred yards on the left. Otherwise, **turn R** (signposted Mottram St Andrew) and soon **turn L** (Oak Road – signposted Mottram St Andrew). The lane eventually descends, with fine views of the distant Greater Manchester high rise buildings across the plain and passing the Peter Pownall wood design workshops on the right. **Turn L** (signposted Alderley Edge) at the T-junction in Mottram St Andrew, noting the bench seat circling the tree to the right, a product of the workshops and an excellent picnic spot. Almost immediately **turn R** (Wilmslow Old Road – signposted Wilmslow) to descend to the A538. Here **turn R** (signposted Prestbury) and very soon **turn L** (signposted Adlington Hall). **Turn R** at the crossroads (signposted Prestbury, B5358) and first **turn L** (Mill Lane – first signposted Macclesfield Avoiding Low Bridge, then Adlington), to eventually pass Adlington Hall on the right and view the high moorlands of Lyme Park ahead.

Go over the A523 at the traffic lights by the Legh Arms and climb gradually to cross the Middlewood Way and Macclesfield Canal, where **immediately turn R** (Sugar Lane – signposted Bollington). Soon note White Nancy on the hill ahead. We cross the Macclesfield Canal once more and descend steeply to **turn R** into Adlington Road car park.

• •

BOLLINGTON

This little town grew up alongside the Macclesfield Canal. Cotton mills and coal mines were built, which now have been replaced by smaller businesses and, with the increased popularity of hill walking, cycling, boating and horse riding, tourism has become an important industry. Impossible to miss, White Nancy, standing on top of Kerridge Hill, overlooks the town. This is a brilliantly whitewashed, 15 foot high hollow dome, built about 1815 by the Gaskell family.

Opinions vary as to the origin of the name; Nancy was the name of the builder's wife and daughter and also one of the horses which dragged a massive stone table top up the hill to be installed inside the folly. Additionally, there used to be an ordnance survey column on the site and 'Nancy' could be a corruption of 'ordnance'.

GAWSWORTH HALL

The original Norman house was rebuilt in 1480. The notorious Mary Fitton, possibly the Dark Lady of Shakespeare's sonnets, lived here. Her career at the court of Queen Elizabeth I ended when, following an affair with the Earl of Pembroke, she was sent to the Tower of London. The Fitton finances never recovered and after many legal battles, in 1712, Lord Mohun and the Duke of Hamilton fought over the estates in the most famous duel in English history and both were killed. Information: 01260 223456. www.gawsworthhall.com

HENBURY HALL

A recent building in the style of Palladio's Villa Rotunda of 1552, on the site of old Henbury Hall. For a real treat, cycle past the grounds in late spring when the famed bluebells are in flower.

ADLINGTON HALL

The home of the Leghs of Adlington since 1315. The Great Hall contains a 17th century organ, which was played by Handel. The gardens were landscaped in the style of Capability Brown in the mid 18th century. Visitors may walk through the wilderness area with its wide variety of trees, azaleas and rhododendrons. Recent additions include a maze and water garden.

Bollington, Macclesfield Forest and Wildboarclough

22 miles

This hilly ride from Bollington, north of Macclesfield, skirts the gritstone edges of the Pennines to reveal breathtaking views over the Cheshire Plain. Descending to Langley we turn, alongside Ridgegate Reservoir, through the Macclesfield Forest and up into the high moorland of the Peak District National Park and thence to Danebridge on the Staffordshire border. The return is a long gentle climb through Wildboarclough, a spectacularly steep dip to the wildfowl haven of Lamaload Reservoir, and some steep little climbs to regain the western edges of the Peak. A possible detour of 5 miles to take in the noted viewpoint of Pym's Chair on the Derbyshire border is shown on the map.

Maps: OS Landranger 118 Stoke-on-Trent & Macclesfield (GR 931781).

Starting point: Adlington Road car park, Bollington (note the evening closing time displayed). *By car:* from the A523 Stockport/Macclesfield road, turn east just north of Macclesfield, signposted Bollington. *By train:* Prestury Station, 2 miles west. *By cycle:* from routes 6 and 7.

Refreshments: The Redway Tavern at Kerridge, the St Dunston Inn in Langley, Leather's Smithy Inn by Ridgegate Reservoir, the Hanging Gate at Higher Sutton, the Ship Inn at Wincle and the Crag at Wildboarclough.

The route: Hilly lanes throughout, with many steep, twisting, narrow lanes, so low gears and good brakes are needed.

Turn R out of the car park and **turn L** at the T-junction (Palmerston Street), past the Dog and Partridge, and almost immediately **turn R** (signposted Cheshire Cycleway) to ascend over the Macclesfield Canal. **Turn L** at the T-junction (signposted Cheshire Cycleway, soon signed Jackson Lane) and at the top of the hill, just after the Bulls Head pub, **turn L** (Redway – signposted

Cheshire Cycleway) and pass the Redway Tavern, noting the old inn sign and poem on the wall.

The road becomes Windmill Lane and climbs steeply with magnificent views, first over Bollington and later over Macclesfield and the Cheshire Plain. Soon after the lane becomes Kerridge Road, **turn L** (Lidgetts Lane) to climb out of the woodland

41

Wildboarclough

into open pasture and heathland bordered by dry gritstone walls.

Turn R at the T-junction, leaving the cycleway, and very soon **turn L** (Calrofold Lane). **Turn L** at the T-junction and soon **turn R** (both unsignposted). Then over the crossroads (Back Eddisbury Road). **Turn L** at the crossroad (unsignposted) and immediately **turn R** (Broadcar Road) which eventually becomes a narrow, steep, winding descent to Langley.

Turn L at the T-junction (soon signposted Macclesfield Forest, Main Road), past the St Dunston Inn on the left and a colourful

village sign on the right. Leaving the village, the craggy hill, seen left across the reservoir, is Tegg's Nose. Pass Leather's Smithy Inn on the left to enter Macclefield Forest and ride alongside Ridgegate Reservoir on the right. Cross the head of the reservoir and Trentabank Reservoir lies around the corner to the left but we **turn R** (Higher Sutton and Wincle) for a steep climb out of the woods onto high moorland.

Turn L at a T-junction (unsignposted) passing the Hanging Gate pub on the right and entering the Peak District National Park. Now there are hilly views on all sides, notably Croker Hill to the

42

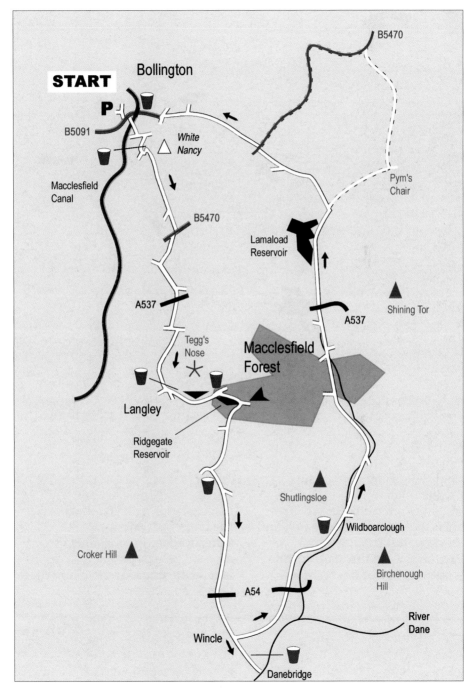

The descent to Lamaload Reservoir

right and Shutlingsloe to the left. Go straight over the crossroads (signposted Wincle) and soon descend to Wincle in the lovely Dane Valley, where you look left to see the Hanging Stone, a distant gritstone outcrop, and soon the oddly named Ship Inn, which offers a room for outdoor folk and children. Just beyond is Danebridge, on the Staffordshire border, a popular beauty spot.

Turn R out of the Ship to retrace uphill and **turn R** in front of Wincle church (signposted Wildboarclough). The road climbs steeply and then descends towards Clough Brook. Go straight over the crossroads and follow the lane and brook through the delightfully wooded Wildboarclough, passing the Crag Inn on the left.

Turn L at the T-junction opposite the Stanley Arms (signposted Macclesfield), and go straight over the crossroads (signposted Saltersford and Goyt Valley) to descend an exceptionally steep lane, with stunning views ahead, to Lamaload Reservoir.

*To add a real climb to this ride, you can opt for a detour which adds 5 miles to the route. **Turn R** after passing Lamaload Reservoir (Saltersford) and continue up past*

Jenkin's Chapel to Pym's Chair, a splendid viewpoint on the Derbyshire border. Here either retrace or **turn L** *to descend past Windgather Rocks on the right, popular with climbers, to Kettleshulme where you* **turn L** *onto the B5470 to rejoin the route, before Rainow, in about 3 miles.*

Otherwise continue, on an easier climb towards Pike Low. Look for the memorial stone on your right where we learn: 'Here John Turner was cast away in a heavy snow storm in the night in or about the year 1755'.

Turn R and **turn L** over the staggered crossroads (signposted Bollington) and descend to the town, where you **turn L** at the T-junction and immediately go straight over the mini-roundabout (signposted Macclesfield), through the traffic lights and under the aqueduct, and **turn R** immediately after the Dog and Partridge (Addlington Road), to soon **turn L** into the car park.

• •

TEGG'S NOSE

For hundreds of years Tegg's Nose was a stone quarry and many streets of Macclesfield were paved with the hard-wearing pink stone which was dressed on site. Quarrying came to an end in 1955 and a host of plants and animals have since established themselves on the cliffs which drop from the harsh 400 metre summit to the sheltered valley 200 metres below. The area is now a country park.

MACCLESFIELD FOREST

A scenic blend of coniferous forest, lakes and species-rich, upland, acid grassland with an extensive variety of wildlife. Managed by Cheshire Wildlife Trust. Toilets and information can be found at Trentabank Reservoir, where there is a heronry of about 22 pairs.

THE SHIP INN

This 16th century inn has a double connection with the sea. The local squire was a keen huntsman, whose friend named an Indiaman cotton trader after him. This ship had a sportsman and two dogs as a figurehead and the squire is said to have returned the compliment by portraying the ship on his inn sign. The ship itself was lost off the Cape of Good Hope in 1862 and the inn sign was replaced in Edwardian times by a picture of the *Nimrod*, presented by the mother of Sir Philip Swythamley. Sir Philip sailed with Shackleton on his 1907 Antarctic expedition and reached 88 degrees south. Having lost two toes to frostbite, he was not in the group which reached the pole but the whole expedition returned as heroes.

JENKIN'S CHAPEL AND PYM'S CHAIR

This lane is known as 'The Street' and was a Roman road, used later by jaggers (packhorsemen) as they travelled from east to west carrying coal and salt to and from Cheshire and Derbyshire. Jenkin is said to have given spiritual support to the jaggers. The site of Pym's Chair was originally situated some 300 metres to the south of the car park at the top of the hill, on the Cheshire/Derbyshire border. Pym has been variously said to have been a highwayman, the leader of a gang of thieves, and a fiery Methodist preacher.

9

Circuit of Congleton
32 miles

This varied route begins on the slopes of The Cloud, a fine viewpoint on the Cheshire-Staffordshire border, and descends to the Macclesfield Canal, whose course we follow as far south as Scholar Green. We strike north at Rode Pool on flat, marginal farmland and heathland, to cross the River Dane, go through the picturesque parkland of Davenport Hall and visit the Quinta. Then east to the grave of Maggoty Johnson, the last official English jester, at Gawsworth Hall, before climbing back onto The Cloud.

Map: OS Landranger 118 Stoke-on-Trent & Macclesfield (GR 894628)

Starting point: Timbersbrook car park. *By car:* from the A54, north of Congleton, turn east (signed picnic area, Middle Lane) and follow the picnic signs to the car park on the left. *By train:* the route passes within ½ mile of Congleton Station. *By cycle:* from routes 7, 10, 11 and 12.

Refreshments: Marton Coffee House and numerous pubs en route, including the Swettenham Arms.

The route: Mostly flat or gently rolling lanes with three hilly miles, two short stretches of A road, plus a mile of tarmac/stone bridleway.

Turn **L** from the car park and **turn R** at the crossroads (Under Rainow Road – signposted Congleton Station). The lane soon descends with views to the right, over the Cheshire Plain to the Welsh hills. Past the Coach and Horses, **turn R** at the T-junction (Reades Lane – signposted Congleton) to descend to Congleton outskirts, passing under the Biddulph Valley Way and over a tributary of the River Dane.

Go straight across the traffic lights (Leek Road) and, before the road bends right over the railway, **turn L** (Moss Road) into open countryside. Again **turn L** immediately before the railway (signed Mow Lane eventually) and before long **turn R** at the Horseshoe Inn (Fence Lane, soon signposted Scholar Green).

The road skirts the hill, becomes Wharf Lane, and then descends. Before the railway, **turn L** (signposted 'no through road') and **bear R** at a fork to cross the railway through bridleway gates (care: look and listen for trains). **Turn L** at the T-junction (unsignposted), soon noting Mow Cop Castle on the hill

Brereton Hall gatehouse

(Wall Hill Lane – signposted Brookhouse Green). Soon, immediately after the Bluebell Inn, **turn R** (unsignposted). **First R** (signposted Brereton) and immediate **turn L** by Brookhouse Green Methodist church (signposted Brereton). **First R** (unsignposted) and straight over the crossroads at the A534 (Smethwick Lane). **Turn L** at the T-junction (unsignposted, eventually Moss Lane), and **turn L** at the T-junction (unsignposted) and **turn R** at the crossroads (Bagmere Lane), passing Brereton Heath Country Park on the right.

Cross the A54 onto the bridleway (signposted as a bridleway, 'no through road'). Through the bridleway gate (signed Davenport Hall) the surface becomes stony (take care). **Keep R** at the fork and the track descends to a second bridleway gate and a bridge over the River Dane. There is a gentle climb to a third gate after which we regain tarmac.

Just before the church, **turn L** into the car park of the Swettenham Arms. To the left and rear of the pub is a gate leading into the Quinta. This is a beautiful spot in which to linger and the pub serves excellent food.

Exit, following the one-way round St Peter's church (see ride 11), and **turn L** at the T-junction by the church (unsignposted). Pass a 'no through road' on the left and soon

to the left, and pass the Heritage Marina on the right to **turn R** at the T-junction (Springbank – signposted Scholar Green). Go over the Macclesfield Canal, and skirt Scholar Green, to **turn L** at the T-junction (signposted Newcastle, A34) and soon take the **first turn R** (signposted Rode Hall Gardens), before long passing the entrance to the gardens. At Rode Pool **turn sharp R** (Chancel Hall Lane) and the full silhouette of Mow Castle is visible.

Approaching the A34 **turn L** (Brook Lane) and **turn L** at the T-junction (unsignposted). At Brownlow Inn crossroads **turn L**

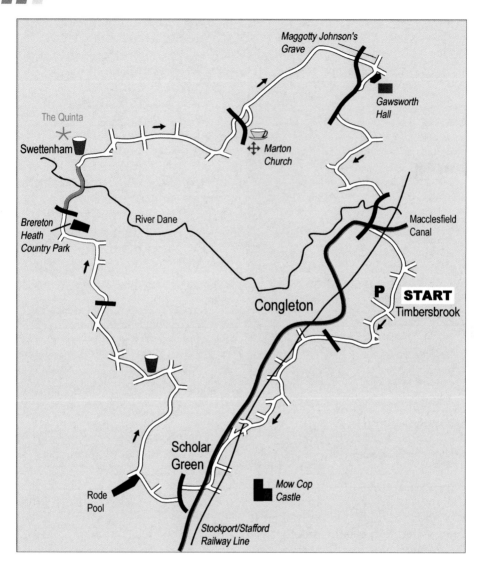

turn L (signed 'deep ford ahead'). You can choose a stone clapper bridge instead of the ford. At the T-junction **turn L** and immediate **turn R** (unsignposted). Go over the crossroads (signposted Marton, eventually Messuage Lane). **Turn L** at a T-junction (Marton Hall Lane – signposted Marton) and **immediately**

turn L at the fork (unsignposted), soon looking right to view Marton's church across the fields.

At the A34, the lane to Gawsworth lies ahead but I suggest **turning R** for 200 yards to visit Marton Coffee House and the church on the left.

Turn **R** out of the Coffee House and **first R** (Oak Lane). **Turn R** at the T-junction (unsignposted), soon passing Marton Heath trout pools on the right. Go straight over the A536 (Maggoty Lane – signposted Sutton) to a crossroads with park on the left by the National Trust sign and gate. A plaque informs us that Maggoty Johnson, 1691-1773, is buried nearby. To view the poem on his gravestone, take the path through the wood for a few yards.

Continuing, **turn R** from the halt (Church Lane – signposted Congleton). After the road bears sharp right, you can view splendid Gawsworth Hall across the lake to the left. The effigies in the Fitton family church, at the far end of the lake, are worth investigation.

Pass the Harrington Arms on the right (soon, families may prefer to go left onto the 'no through road' and take the pavement). **Turn L** at the T-junction (signposted Congleton, A536). First **turn L** (Shellow Lane – signposted North Rode), first **turn R** (Pexhall Lane – signposted Marton), first **turn L** (signposted North Rode) and **turn L** at the T-junction (signposted North Rode). Watch for the old 'Cyclists Ride with Caution' sign on the left.

Turn R at the T-junction (signposted Congleton, A54) to cross the River Dane on a packhorse bridge and ascend to cross the canal, immediately **turning L** (Peover Lane), for the climb to The Cloud. Quarrying in the early 19th century, for the construction of the Macclesfield Canal, left the distinctive edge ahead.

Turn R at the T-junction (Tunstall Road) and descend. At the bottom of a hill the road bends right, with a red telephone box on the left, and we immediately **turn R** (Weathercock Lane) and soon **turn R** into the car park.

• •

TIMBERSBROOK
A pretty parking spot with picnic area, toilets and information board, on the site of the Silversprings Bleaching and Dyeing Company works. From the 1900s, for sixty years, cotton cloth was brought here from Manchester for treatment.

THE OLD MAN OF MOW AND MOW COP CASTLE
Millstone grit has been extracted here since the Iron Age and now the Old Man of Mow (National Trust) stands as a rock pinnacle isolated by quarrying. The castle was built in 1754 as a picturesque folly, to add effect to the eastern skyline as seen from Rode Hall.

MARTON CHURCH
Founded in 1343, the half-timbered, black and white church of St James and St Paul is claimed to be one of the oldest surviving wood and plaster churches in Europe. Curiosities inside include two stone effigies of knights and medieval frescos.

Alderley Edge and the Jodrell Bank Radio Telescope

23 miles

S tarting from Alderley Edge, an isolated Pennine outcrop and local beauty spot, this ride encompasses some of the most prosperous areas of the Cheshire Plain. Traditional features include water mills, black and white timber-frame cottages and imposing halls surrounded by their landscaped parklands. In this setting the vast bowl of Jodrell Bank radio telescope provides a dramatic reminder of the present day.

Map: OS Landranger 118 Stoke-on-Trent & Macclesfield (GR 860773).

Starting point: Alderley Edge National Trust car park. *By car:* from the A34 in Alderley Edge, take the B5087, signed Macclesfield. The car park is on the left almost immediately after The Wizard restaurant. *By train:* Alderley Edge Station is 1½ miles to the north-west, or start from Goostrey Station en route. *By cycle:* from routes 7, 9, 11 and 12.

Refreshments: At Alderley Edge, a snack van in the car park at weekends and school holidays and the Wizard Tea Room. On the route you will find the Stag's Head Hotel in Warford, a café in the Jodrell Bank Visitor Centre (admission charge) and the Red Lion pub in nearby Goostrey.

The route: Flat or gently rolling lanes, with a total of ½ mile of A road and about a mile of firmly surfaced bridleway. One long gradual climb at the finish, to regain Alderley Edge.

Turn **R** out of the car park and **immediately turn L** opposite the Wizard (Artists' Lane – signposted Chelford) to descend through mature woodland and past charming timber-frame and thatched cottages. At the A34 crossroads a diversion left is possible to Nether Alderley Water Mill (600 yards); otherwise cross the road, noting the butter cross stump ahead (Welsh Row –

signposted Chelford), to continue.

At the T-junction **turn R** (signposted Alderley Edge, A535) and in about 600 yards **turn L** (Merryman's Lane – signposted Great Warford). Before long look ahead and right for a white memorial stone in a graveyard which heralds the approach of Norbury House, an attractive Baptist chapel dated 1642. Soon

Birtles octagonal church tower

the little bridge to look through the grilled window of Bate Mill to see the undershot water wheel.

Ahead, on the climb from this idyllic spot, the dramatic bowl of the telescope appears again. **Turn R** at the T-junction (unsigned) and you will pass the entrance to the Visitor Centre. Continue to Goostrey, **turning L** at the T-junction by the church (signposted Twemlow Green), passing the Red Lion pub on the left.

Turn L at the next T-junction and immediately **turn L** onto the A535 at Twemlow Green, then **immediately turn R** (Forty Acre Lane – signposted Swettenham). Keep an eye open to the right and in about ½ mile, immediately after a zigzag road sign, **turn R**, opposite a bridleway sign, through the gateposts of Kermincham Hall onto a tarmac road. Take care as there are two drainage gullies across this road which bends left and right past a farmyard and then left past attractive properties to a bridleway gate. Through the gate the road is unsealed but the surface is firm. Through a second gate we enter the Swettenham Meadows Nature Reserve, 21 acres of species-rich grassland, ponds and woodland managed by the Cheshire Wildlife Trust.

Before long the road becomes tarmac again and we **turn R** at the crossroads (unsigned) and **second L** (signposted Swettenham Heath). **Turn L** at the T-junction (unsigned)

after Warford Hall on the left, **turn L** (signposted David Lewis Centre) to pass the Stags Head Hotel with its tempting, south-facing cobbled forecourt, on the right.

Pass the David Lewis Centre in Little Warford and continue to Marthall. Here cross the A537 (Sandhole Lane, becomes Snelson Lane). Go straight over the crossroads (Mill Lane, becomes Boundary Lane) and, as Jodrell Bank radio telescope becomes visible on the left, look for a turn and **turn L** (signposted Bate Mill but the post may be hidden in summer). After passing under a railway bridge we descend to the river, the oddly named Peover Eye, where it is worthwhile stopping at

and over the crossroads (signposted Marton), then first **turn L** by the pond (Hodgehill Lane – signposted Siddington Heath). Note the grisly arms of the Davenport family, painted black and white, on the house wall ahead. Go over the crossroads (Colshaw Lane – signposted Siddington), to the T-junction where you **turn R** on the B5392 (signposted Siddington). **Turn L** at the T-junction (signposted Manchester, A34) for

about 400 yards (families may prefer to use the pavement) and take the second **turn R** (Fanshawe Lane – signposted Henbury) past Redesmere (go carefully, wildfowl wander on the road) on a fine rolling single track lane.

Take the **first L** (signposted Chelford) past the splendid bluebell and rhododendron woods of Henbury Hall. Go over the crossroads (Birtles Lane –

Jodrell Bank radio telescope

ALDERLEY EDGE

Alderley Edge is an isolated 600 foot red sandstone escarpment with views over the Cheshire Plain and the Pennines. The Romans mined copper here, and there are remains of mine shafts and tunnels in the woods. The wizard who gave his name to the restaurant is said to have bought a horse from a local farmer to provide a steed for one of the soldiers who sleeps under the hill, ready to awaken in times of England's need.

NETHER ALDERLEY WATER MILL

A National Trust property dating from the 15th century, unusual in possessing overshot tandem wheels. The mill stones are French burrs, made up from pieces of a quartz rock, bound in iron hoops and backed with plaster of Paris. French burr is very hard and can grind up to 100 tons of grain before dressing. The machinery was in use until 1939, after which it lay derelict. It was given to the National Trust in 1950 and restored to working order in 1967 and now gives regular flour-grinding demonstrations. Admission charge.

JODRELL BANK RADIO TELESCOPE

The Visitor Centre includes an astronomy and physics exhibition with a planetarium, an arboretum, an environmental discovery centre, and a café and adventure playground. Admission charge.

HARE HILL

A National Trust woodland garden with azaleas, rhododendrons and a walled garden with wire sculptures. Entry free to NT members.

signposted Birtles) soon noting the gear wheels and mill stones of the old Birtle Mill set in the wall to the right. Passing Birtles Hall on the left, climb gradually past St Catherine's church with its unusual octagonal tower to a staggered crossroads, by the Black Greyhound Smithy, where you **turn R** and **turn L** onto a narrow lane (signposted Prestbury, Mottram St Andrew) to descend to a T-junction. Here **turn L** (signposted Alderley Edge but hidden on the right) past the Hare Hill estate. **Turn R** before the 'No Entry' sign and **turn R** at the T-junction (unsignposted), taking the B5087 for ½ mile to **turn R** into the Alderley Edge NT car park.

Holmes Chapel, Swettenham and Peover

23 miles

This route uses four short stretches of bridleway to view historic inns, timber-frame churches, and ancient manors. We commence at Holmes Chapel and before long turn onto the first bridleway past Brereton Hall. To cross the beautiful Dane Valley, we take to the grounds of Davenport Hall. Then, through or around a deep ford, we turn west to Goostrey village, Peover Hall and the famous Bells of Peover, returning on a bridleway past the Hermitage, a remote country house.

> **Map:** OS Landranger 118 Stoke-on-Trent & Macclesfield (GR 763672).
>
> **Starting point:** Holmes Chapel village centre. *By car:* The village centre car park is on the east side of the A50, south of the church, in Holmes Chapel. *By train:* from Holmes Chapel Station. *By cycle:* from routes 9, 10 and 12.
>
> **Refreshments:** The Swettenham Arms, the Bear's Head Inn at Brereton Green, the Red Lion in Goostrey and the Bells of Peover.
>
> **The route:** Flat and gently rolling lanes with about 4 miles of bridleway.

Turn **R** out of the car park and turn **L** at the mini-roundabouts (Middlewich Road – signposted Middlewich). Take the second turn **L** (Brookfield Drive), turn **R** at the T-junction, immediately turn **L** (Grassmere Drive) and very soon turn **R** (Conistone Drive). **Turn L** at the T-junction into open country (unsignposted).

Go over the M6 and eventually turn **L** at the T-junction (unsignposted, later signposted Brereton Green). Go over the M6 again and over the railway. At a staggered crossroads **turn R** and turn **L**, passing the Bear's Head Inn

on the left, and very soon **turn L** (signposted 'church', and 'no through road'), through a gatehouse, into the grounds of Brereton Hall. **Bear R** at the fork (signposted as a public path), glimpsing Brereton Hall, a Grade 1 listed Elizabethan house, in the woods to the left, and then St Oswald's church.

Soon the road bends left. **Turn R** here onto an unsealed road (waymarked as a public path) through a gate. Through a second gate the road becomes smooth, crushed stone. **Turn L** at the crossroads, soon passing Brereton

Peover church, a mixture of sandstone and timber frame

Heath Country Park entrance on the right.

Go straight over the crossroads onto a bridleway (signposted as a bridleway, 'no through road'). Through the bridleway gate (signed Davenport Hall) there are a few yards of loose gravel (take care). **Keep R** at the fork and the track descends through parkland to a second bridleway gate and a bridge over the lovely River Dane. There is a gentle climb to a third gate to regain tarmac.

In Swettenham village, note St Peter's church on the left. Stop at the little war memorial and look back to view the ass's head effigy above the north door and the Swettenham Arms, a 16th century inn, originally a nunnery which provided travellers with accommodation.

Very soon pass a 'no through road' and shortly afterwards **turn L** (signed 'deep ford ahead'). You can choose a stone clapper bridge instead of the ford. At the T-junction **turn L** (unsignposted), soon passing the Kermincham village sign. **Turn L** at the T-junction (Forty Acre Lane – signposted Twemlow Green), noting the Jodrell Bank radio telescope ahead.

Turn L at the T-junction (signposted Holmes Chapel, A535), and immediately **turn R** (signposted Cranage), immediately **turning R** again (signposted Goostrey). Entering Goostrey, pass the Red Lion and St Luke's church on the right and immediately **turn R** (Church Bank – signposted Blackden Heath). Take the first **turn L** (Blackden Lane – signposted Blackden Heath).

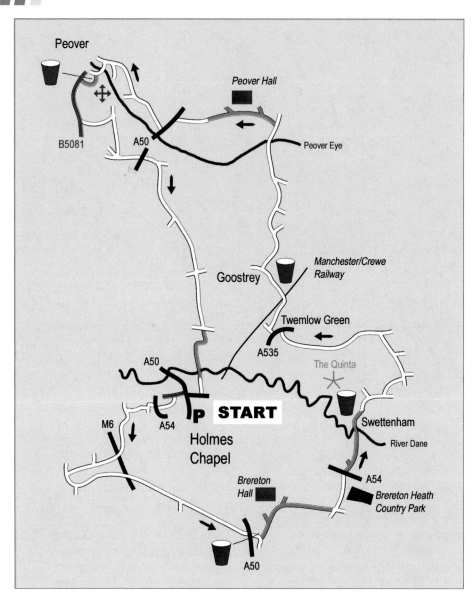

Eventually the road dips to cross the Peover Eye brook and climbs past woodland. Soon **turn L** through white gateposts into the grounds of Peover Hall (signposted as a bridleway, 'private road'). First

fork L (signposted as a bridleway), and **keep left** through a bridleway gate (signposted as a bridleway) onto a green lane, soon cobbled, through woodland and onto tarmac. Eventually **turn L** at a

The clapper bridge by Swettenham ford

T-junction (unsignposted, A50), soon **turning R** (Free Green Lane – signposted Lower Peover).

Pass Mill Lane and Foxcovert Lane on the left, then **turn L** (unsignposted), just after a small postbox and between the road signs for Free Green Lane and Broom Lane. Very soon **turn L** (Barrows Brow – signposted 'School'). Cross the Peover Eye and **keep L** on Church Walk to the churchyard. Here dismount and go through the bridleway gate to approach the lovely black and white church of St Oswald. Opposite the church tower, **turn R** to visit the Bells of Peover with its ancient wisteria.

Retrace to the church tower, continue through the churchyard, remounting to descend The Cobbles. **Turn L** at the T-junction onto the B5081 (unsignposted). Pass the Crown Inn on the right and take the first **turn L** (Foxcovert Lane). **Turn R** at the T-junction (Heath Lane). **Turn L** at the T-junction (Townfield Lane) and go over the crossroads (Booth Bed Lane) eventually signposted Goostrey.

Go over the crossroads in Goostrey (Hermitage Lane). Continue over the next crossroads and through stone gate posts (signed 'no through road', 'bridle and foot path'). The road bends right to pass Hermitage Farm. **Turn L** in front of Hollins Farm entrance onto an unsealed road which descends to cross the River Dane on a cobbled bridge and ascends steeply to Holmes Chapel. Through the gate posts, continue straight ahead on Hermitage Drive. **Turn R** at the T-junction (unsignposted) onto the A535. **Turn L** at the mini-roundabout (signposted Kidsgrove), past the church and Old Red Lion and **turn L** into the village centre.

HOLMES CHAPEL

This was a tiny village which grew rapidly after the opening of the Crewe to Manchester railway line in 1842. Dimples on the north side of the church tower are cited as evidence of musket fire during a skirmish in the square between Royalists and Parliamentarians in 1643.

THE BEAR'S HEAD INN

This early 17th century timber-frame inn takes its name from the local Brereton family's arms. The family tree begins in 1175 with William de Brereton. It is said that a valet rudely interrupted him at dinner and, seeing his master's anger, fled upstairs but Sir William pursued him and murdered him. Sir William, in fear of the consequences, went to London to plead for pardon with the king, who refused at first but then offered him a challenge. He said he would allow Sir William three days in which to invent a muzzle for a bear. Sir William was shut up in the Tower and at the end of that time was brought before a bear which was let loose. The prisoner flung a newly invented leather muzzle over its head and escaped unharmed. From that time the muzzled bear became the emblem of the Breretons.

BRERETON HEATH COUNTRY PARK

Until 1959 this wooded heathland was managed for timber and game. Then sand was extracted and the lake which was left now forms the centre of Brereton Heath Country Park. Facilities include a car park, pathways open to cyclists, an information centre and toilets.

SWETTENHAM AND THE QUINTA

First mentioned 1304, the original timber-frame church, St Peter's, has sandstone and brick additions. The effigy of a donkey was placed there by a lord of the Mainwarings who, when fighting in the Crusades, had his horse shot from under him and continued on an ass. The Quinta, behind the Swettenham Arms, comprises new plantation, ancient mixed woodland, unimproved grassland, water features and an arboretum with over 5,000 specimen trees and shrubs. The Cheshire Wildlife Trust has bought the land, once owned by Sir Bernard Lovell. Access is open.

PEOVER

St Oswald's half-timbered church dates from 1269 and has a red sandstone tower built in 1582. The Bells of Peover, which dates back 500 years, flies the Stars and Stripes because this inn was a regular meeting place for Eisenhower and Patton during the Second World War, when Peover Hall was at their disposal. The hall is an Elizabethan house, dating from 1585, in an 18th century landscaped park.

Hassall Green: A circuit of Sandbach

19 miles

This circuit of Sandbach is probably the flattest ride that can be imagined and only a few miles near the start have any gradient. The landscape is of pasturage, enlivened by the colourful gardens of numerous isolated farms and cottages, with a variety of water features, of which only the brooks are natural. We commence by traversing the Trent & Mersey Canal, completed in 1777, which we cross again on the outskirts of Middlewich. To the south of this 'salt town' we become increasingly aware of road subsidence and finally encounter some 'flashes', large shallow pools, these days a haven for wildlife, created by hasty, and now defunct, methods of salt extraction. Finally we return via Winterley Pool which once powered a water mill.

Map: OS Landranger 118 Stoke-on-Trent & Macclesfield (GR 775583).

Starting point: The Salt Line car park, 2 miles north-west of Alsager. *By car:* from the A533, north of Alsager, turn west, signposted Hassall Green, Canal Centre and Potter's Barn. The car park is on the right, after the canal and immediately after passing under the motorway. *By train:* Alsager Station is approximately 3 miles south-west. *By cycle:* from routes 9, 11 and 13.

Refreshments: Brindley's Lockside Restaurant and the Romping Donkey pub in Hassall Green and the Bear's Head in Brereton Green.

The route: Quiet lanes, rolling slightly for a few miles in the Hassall area but otherwise entirely flat.

Turn L out of the car park (unsignposted, eventually signposted Smallwood), under the motorway and soon over the Trent & Mersey Canal, with locks to the left and right and, immediately on the right, Brindley's Lockside Restaurant. Soon we pass the Romping Donkey pub and, though it is not signposted, we leave the National Cycle Route (NCR) 5, on which we have been riding. The

distant view ahead and right is of the Mow Cop folly castle.

Go over the crossroads at the New Inn (Love Lane – signposted Smallwood), over the next crossroads at the traffic lights (signposted Smallwood) and, immediately after the little St John the Baptist church, **turn L** (School Lane). Before long pass Old Farm, a black and white timber building

Winterley Pool

with brick extensions, on the left and Overton Hall Farm on the right and soon after **turn R** (unsignposted). **Turn R** at the T-junction (unsignposted, eventually signed Mill Lane) and over a little stream, and **turn R** at a T-junction again (unsignposted) and immediately **turn L** (unsignposted, Farriers Cottage sign on the gate). **Turn L** at the crossroads (unsignposted, eventually signed Moss End Lane). Go over a crossroads (Moorhead Lane – signposted Brereton). **Turn R** at the T-junction (unsignposted) to pass the Brereton Green Millennium Garden outside the gateposts of Brereton Hall and then the Bear's Head Inn, dated 1615, on the right.

Turn R at the T-junction and immediately **turn L** (Back Lane, eventually signposted Sproston). Over the railway and motorway the lane becomes Brereton Lane. **Turn L** (Jones Lane – signposted Hollinsgreen), soon **turn R** (Cledford Lane – signposted Cledford) and **turn R** immediately after a large farm (signposted Cledford Lane). The factory, seen ahead and left across the fields, is a salt factory. Before long we pass a Middlewich sign and go under a railway and over the Trent & Mersey Canal to a crossroads, where the route is straight across (Cross Lane) into the outskirts of the town. **Turn L** at the T-junction (Warmingham Lane) and, though it is not signposted, we are again on

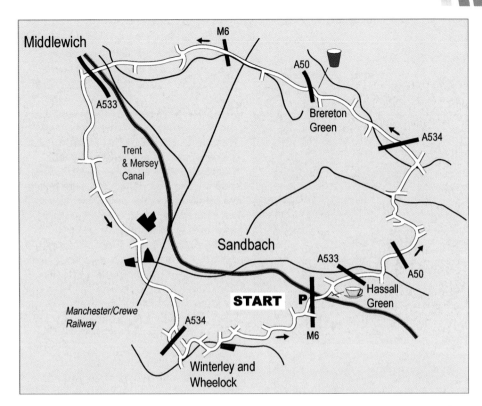

NCR 5. Out into open country, past a Moston sign, though no village is visible, and **turn L** at the T-junction (Forge Mill Lane) and soon **turn R** (signposted White Hall Lane – signposted Warmingham) leaving NCR 5.

Enter Warmingham and soon **turn L** (Crab Mill Road) to pass isolated, charming little cottages and farms on a road which is liable to subsidence, since we are in a Cheshire salt mining area. Over the crossroads (Clay Lane) there are salt flashes on both sides of the road, which are popular with bird watchers. **Turn R** immediately before the busy A534

(unsignposted), soon **turn L** at the T-junction (signposted Haslington), go over the A road on a bridge and immediately **turn L** (Clay Lane – signposted Winterley and Wheelock Heath).

Turn R at a T-junction (Kents Green Lane) and **turn L** at a T-junction into Winterley and Wheelock Heath and soon, past a warning of wildfowl and round the corner, we cross the retaining wall of Winterley Pool, which extends on the right. An interesting identification board details the wildlife to be seen.

Turn R at the far end of the pool

Cyclists and boaters at Hassall Green

(Pool Lane), **turn R** at the crossroads (signposted Hassall, Hassall Road) and **turn R** at the T-junction (signposted Hassall and Hassall Green) to pass 'Get Ahead Hats' at School Farm. Just before the motorway, opposite Station House, **turn L** into the Salt Line car park.

● ●

THE TRENT & MERSEY CANAL

Originally known as the Grand Trunk Canal, the Trent & Mersey runs 93 miles from Derwent Mouth, where it joins the River Trent, to Preston Brook, where it joins a branch of the Bridgewater Canal which links to the Mersey. It was to be part of the Grand Cross, a scheme to link the four rivers Trent, Mersey, Severn and Thames, and was engineered by James Brindley, until his death in 1772.

HASSALL GREEN

This little hamlet lies halfway up 'Heartbreak Hill', the thirty locks that lift the canal from the Cheshire Plain to Harecastle Hill near Stoke-on-Trent. The shop and house by the locks were built at the same time as the canal and the shop has catered for working boatmen and now holiday boats for nearly two centuries; the present shop building used to be the local bakery and stables. Newly-built Brindley's Restaurant next door offers fine views over the canal.

SALT FLASHES

From Roman times saturated brine from natural springs that welled up around this area of Cheshire was collected and evaporated in open pans over a fire to retrieve salt crystals. By the 19th century there were scores of small salt producing companies operating, many still employing extraction methods which had evolved in the Middle Ages and which involved the indiscriminate dissolving of underground salt deposits. As a result, the areas around Cheshire's traditional salt producing towns, the Wiches, were notorious for subsidence caused by this 'wild brine' method; buildings would collapse and the land sink to form what many years later have become picturesque lakes or flashes.

Hassall Green: The South-East Corner

26 or 29 miles

This atypical little corner of rural Cheshire, south of Crewe, has many of the characteristics of neighbouring Staffordshire. Look for early 19th century Primitive Methodist chapels in the hamlets and a greater use of brick in the older farms and cottages. We start on the Circuit of Sandbach route but turn south on a bridleway to skim the outskirts of Alsager and visit the White Lion at Barthomley. Through Englesea-brook, with its museum of Primitive Methodism, we pass briefly into Staffordshire to ride an old toll road through Betley, before turning west and back into Cheshire to join the Cheshire Cycleway at Hatherton. Through Wybunbury, with its solitary leaning church tower, we return through the hamlets of Hough and Winterley.

Map: OS Landranger 118 Stoke-on-Trent & Macclesfield (GR 775583).

Starting point: The Salt Line car park, 2 miles north-west of Alsager. *By car:* from the A533, north of Alsager, turn west, signposted Hassall Green, Canal Centre and Potter's Barn. The car park is on the right, after the canal and almost immediately after passing under the motorway. *By train:* Alsager Station is approximately 3 miles south-west. *By cycle:* from route 12.

Refreshments: The Collector's Kitchen in Dagfields Craft and Antique Centre, the White Lion, Barthomley, the Blue Bell in Wrinehill and the Boar's Head just south of Wybunbury.

The route: 20 miles of gently rolling lanes with just over a mile of bridleway and about 3 miles of B road and 2 miles of A road. The detour to Bridgemere involves short stretches of A road and a lane.

Turn **R** out of the car park, entering the parish of Hassall, and pass a left turn to Day Green and a right turn to Wheelock, cross a small brook and on the next rise turn **L** (unsignposted). Soon **bear L** (signposted bridleway) onto a lumpy tarmac lane which becomes firm stone and earth after the motorway bridge. **Turn R** at the T-junction (Close Lane) on the outskirts of Alsager and take the first through road **turning R** (Nursery Road).

Go over the motorway, and past woodland, on a narrow, winding lane to Oakhanger where there is no village sign but a four-ways with a red traditional telephone box in

The White Lion, Barthomley

the middle. Here **turn L** (signposted Barthomley), passing little St Luke's church on the right. Go over the crossroads onto a narrow lane (signposted 'level crossing 360 yards') and follow the instructions to cross the railway. **Turn L** at the T-junction (signposted Barthomley). At the next T-junction our route lies to the right (signposted Weston and Betley) but first **turn L** for a few hundred yards to view, or perhaps to enter, the lovely White Lion Inn opposite the church of St Bertoline in Barthomley. Retrace and continue, passing the very fine Old Hall Farm on the right. In the next hamlet, cross Englesea Brook and, after the road bends left, look left

for the Primitive Methodist chapel and museum, dated 1828.

Soon we enter Staffordshire. Go over the crossroads (Post Office Lane) and at the T-junction **turn L** (Newcastle Road), passing Doddlespool Hall on the right; go through Betley with its many fine old buildings, eventually passing the Hand and Trumpet on the right and reaching the Blue Bell. This inn has an interesting board listing the Wrinehill tolls, dating from the reign of George IV, on display in the bar. Immediately after the Blue Bell **turn R** (Checkley Lane – signposted Checkley), soon regaining Cheshire and eventually crossing Checkley Brook and passing Checkley Hall on the right.

There is a possible detour at the next crossroads. Either continue straight over (Bridgemere School – signposted Hunterson), noting the Victorian postbox in the wall on the right, or, to visit Bridgemere Garden World, **turn L** onto the main road. In a few hundred yards a **turn L** avoids the main road until just before the gardens.

Continuing on the main route; if you appreciate lovely parkland, look for the sign on the right to St John's church, Doddington, and detour into the grounds of Doddington Hall, a large 18th century private mansion set in gardens landscaped by Capability Brown. The little early 19th century church is in a lovely

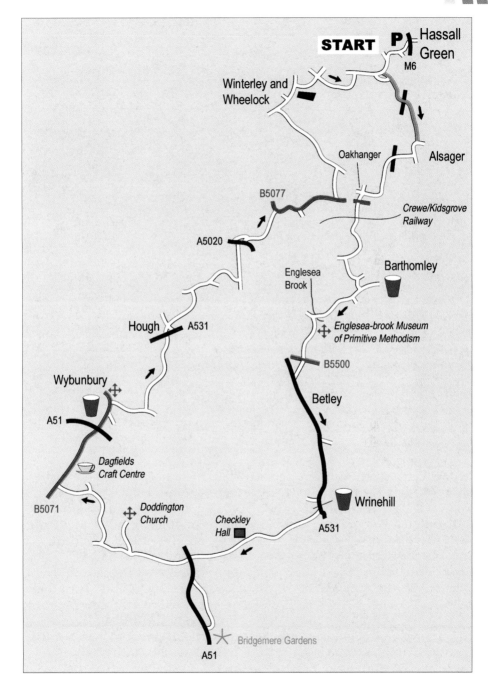

START P Hassall Green

M6

Winterley and Wheelock

Oakhanger

Alsager

B5077

Crewe/Kidsgrove Railway

A5020

Englesea Brook

Barthomley

Hough A531

Englesea-brook Museum of Primitive Methodism

B5500

Wybunbury

Betley

A51

Dagfields Craft Centre

B5071

Doddington Church

Checkley Hall

Wrinehill

A531

Bridgemere Gardens

A51

Englesea-brook chapel and museum

setting. Retrace and continue, taking the first **turn R** (signposted Nantwich). At the crossroads **turn R** (signposted Wybunbury) and soon pass (or visit) Dagfields Craft and Antique Centre on the right. This is open seven days a week, entry is free, there are lots of curios to see, and a café.

To continue go straight over the crossroads at the Boar's Head (signposted Wybunbury). Entering Wybunbury, **turn R** just in front of the church tower (Wrinehill Road – signposted Betley). Take the first **turn L** (Cobbs Lane – signposted Hough). Go through Hough, noting another Primitive Methodist chapel, and over the crossroads (signposted Basford) and immediately over the second crossroads (Casey Lane). **Turn R** at a T-junction (Weston Lane becomes Whites Lane). **Turn L** at a T-junction (signposted Crewe). At the next T-junction, with the busy A5020, go straight across the road, and slightly left, onto a path which in a few yards leads to a road.

Follow this road on the outskirts of Crewe Hall, keeping right, to a T-junction where you **turn L** (Old Park Road). **Turn R** at the T-junction (signposted Alsager, Barthomley Road).

Just before the Oakhanger village sign **turn sharp L**. **Turn L** at the next T-junction (unsignposted). **Turn R** at the T-junction opposite Winterley House (Holmshaw Lane). Go into Winterley and Wheelock Heath and soon, past a warning of wildfowl and around the corner, cross the retaining wall of Winterley Pool which extends on the right. **Turn R** at the far end of the pool (Pool Lane), **turn R** at the crossroads (Hassall Road – signposted Hassall) and **turn R** at the T-junction (signposted Hassall and Hassall Green) to pass 'Get Ahead Hats' at School Farm. Just before the motorway, opposite Station House, **turn L** into the Salt Line car park.

● ●

THE SALT LINE

The original railway, built in the mid 19th century, carried minerals to and from Stoke-on-Trent. Now this short line, which connects with the Trent & Mersey Canal towpath, is a trail open to walkers, cyclists and horse riders.

BARTHOMLEY

An attractive village, which was the scene of a major battle during the Civil War. Opposite the sandstone church, the black and white, timber-framed, thatched pub dates from 1614 and is surrounded by charming Jacobean cottages with attractive gardens. Most of the farmhouses in the area were built by Lord Crewe in the early part of the 19th century and have large cheeserooms, usually over the kitchen, where the famous Cheshire cheeses dried and matured.

ENGLESEA-BROOK MUSEUM OF PRIMITIVE METHODISM

The old chapel, built in 1828, has been opened as a museum of Primitive Methodism, depicting this 19th century religion which was started in The Potteries. It was one of the settings for Alan Garner's *Red Shift* (1973). Free admission. Information: 01270 820836 or 01782 810109.

BRIDGEMERE GARDEN WORLD

A huge garden centre which offers over 20 different styles of garden, many of which are Chelsea Gold Medal winners: a French rose garden, a woodland setting, a Victorian design, the Women's Institute's cottage and folly gardens, and a rock and water area.

WYBUNBURY

This village is best known for its leaning church tower which is all that remains of the parish church. The chancel was demolished because of structural problems caused by the sandy soil. The tower developed a dangerous list and was underpinned in 1989 to make it safe.

14

Audlem, Wrenbury and Hack Green Secret Bunker

20 miles

There are no real climbs on this ride which begins in the charming little town of Audlem, on the Shropshire Union Canal, and rises imperceptibly to Coxbank near the top lock of the Audlem flight. From here we turn west to Aston, passing The Firs pottery workshops, and Wrenbury, to visit the Dusty Miller pub on the Llangollen Arm of the Shropshire Union Canal. Turning east we take a look at Hack Green Secret Bunker, now a not-so-secret museum of the 'Cold War' period, before swinging south, again over the main arm of the Shropshire Union, to view Audlem Wharf. Throughout we are on narrow lanes in typical Cheshire pastureland, mainly given over to dairy cattle and horses

Maps: OS Landranger 118 Stoke-on-Trent & Macclesfield, with just a few yards on 117 Chester & Wrexham (GR 658436).

Starting point: The car park in Audlem. *By car:* the car park is in Audlem town centre on the A529, just north of its junction with the A525, on the left heading north. *By train:* join the route at Wrenbury Station. *By cycle:* this route links to route 18.

Refreshments: The Old Priest House Café opposite the church in Audlem is a favourite cyclists' rendezvous. There are interesting pubs at Audlem canal wharf and the Paradise mini-brewery and Dusty Miller in Wrenbury. The café at Hack Green is normally only open to museum customers but if they are not busy you may be allowed to use their facilities.

The Route: It is difficult to imagine a flatter ride. There are just over 18 miles of lanes and approximately 1½ miles of quiet, rural A road through Audlem.

Turn **R** out of the car park (unsignposted), soon **turn L** at the T-junction (The Square – signposted A525 Newcastle). On the left is the church, market hall and bear stone and, opposite the church, Beaman's shop, behind which is the lovely little Old Priest House Café. Leave the village on the A525 and in about a mile **turn R** (Paddock Lane – signposted Kinsey Heath). Take the first **turn R** (Wood Orchard Lane – signposted 'weight limit 5.7 tonnes') and **turn R** at the T-junction (unsignposted). The road descends slightly to cross a bridge (look for the brick walls with stone capping) and it is worthwhile stopping to view the magnificent flight of Audlem locks on the right. You might also like to investigate, through the bridleway gate on the left, the fine set of rope marks worn into the iron posts under the bridge. The barge tow ropes, especially when covered in coal dust, were very abrasive.

Continue and soon **turn L** (signposted Coxbank). Soon, immediately after the Jubilee Chapel, **turn R** (unsignposted) and go straight over the crossroads (Heywood Lane).

Turn R at the T-junction (signposted Burleydam) and take the first **turn R** (unsignposted), eventually passing a nicely spruced up timber-frame house. Go straight over the crossroads (Rookery Lane – signposted Aston and Wrenbury). The lane eventually becomes Sheppenhall Lane and we pass a modern thatched house with fanciful pheasants on the roof on the right, eventually entering Aston and passing The Firs pottery on the left. Cross the A530 (signposted Aston and Wrenbury, Micro Brewery) passing the Bhurtpore Inn on the left and, just before Wrenbury Station, the Paradise Brewery and licensed bar, set back from the road on the right.

Turn L at the T-junction in Wrenbury village (Nantwich Road – signposted Cholmondeley,

Cheshire Cycleway), pass the church and Cotton Arms on the right, to arrive at the Wrenbury lift bridge, with the mill on the right and the Dusty Miller on the left.

Turn R out of the Dusty Miller to retrace as far as Wrenbury village, where you continue, passing the village school on the left, to take the second **turn R** (Wrenbury Heath Road – signposted Sound). On reaching a staggered crossroads **turn R** (Sound Lane – signposted Whitchurch and Broomhall) and in a few hundred yards **turn L** (unsignposted). Soon **turn L** at the T-junction and immediately **turn R** (both unsignposted) and soon **turn R** at the next T-junction (unsignposted) and **immediately turn L** (Mickley Hall Lane – signposted 'weak bridge 1 mile ahead').

This road eventually turns sharp left, with a 'no through road' ahead, becoming French Lane. Go over the Shropshire Union Canal and almost immediately **turn R**, past quaint old Hack House, to view Hack Green Secret Nuclear Bunker, usually open at weekends and in school holidays. Note the owl on the radar dish.

Retrace to the lane and **turn R** to continue. **Turn R** at the T-junction (Coole Lane – signposted Audlem). Again we cross the canal and eventually **turn L** at a T-junction (unsignposted) to descend to the River Weaver and then climb slightly to Audlem and the canal.

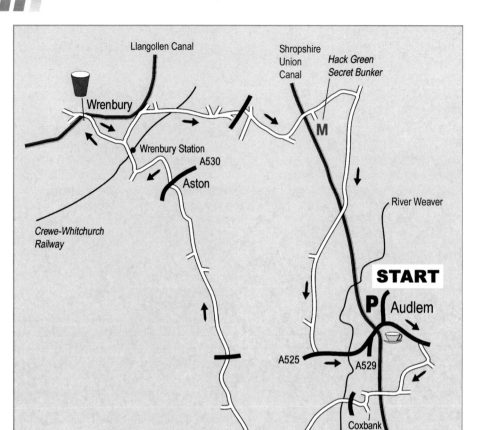

Over the canal, **turn L** before the Bridge Inn to visit Audlem Wharf which has an information board. Retrace to the road to **turn L** and continue, **turning L** in front of the church (signposted Nantwich) and first **turn L** into the car park.

●●●●●●●●●●●●●●●●●●●●●●●●

AUDLEM
This is the most southerly township in Cheshire, the name being a combination of Alda (person's name) and Lyme (forest) as recorded in Domesday Book.

The church of St James was built in 1278 and stands on a large mound in the centre of the village along with the market hall, erected 1733, and beside that the bear stone, a granite boulder probably from Cumberland, deposited by glaciers during the Ice Age, with a ring in it where bears used to be tied for baiting at the local wakes. On the western outskirts of the town, a flight of 15 locks lowers the Shropshire Union Canal almost 100 feet from Shropshire to the Cheshire Plain. The picturesque old wharf is well served with two pubs, the old boatmen's pub, the Bridge, and the Shroppie Fly,

Audlem lock flight

which was originally a warehouse. There is a popular and well-surfaced walk up the towpath beside the lock flight from here.

THE FIRS POTTERY, ASTON

The pottery shop sells a wide variety of thrown and hand-built stoneware pottery. There are weekly one-day pottery workshops for adults and half-day sessions for children. Information: 01270 780345 or www.firspottery.co.uk

HACK GREEN SECRET NUCLEAR BUNKER

This former radar station and Regional Government Headquarters building has been turned into a Cold War museum. You can see a collection of military vehicles, displays relating to radar technology and military communications, a decontamination room, dormitories, Russian defence equipment, BBC office and radio studio, 17,000 gallon water tank, fire and rescue control room, two video theatres, sick bay and NAAFI-style canteen. Even if you do not have time to linger and pay the entry fee, there are interesting exhibits outside and some memorabilia and a video on view in the foyer. Information: 01270 629219 or www.hackgreen.co.uk

Nantwich, Tilstone Bank and Bunbury

23 miles

S tarting from the Venetian Village Marina, north of Nantwich, on the Middlewich branch of the Shropshire Union Canal, this circuit uses some very flat and remote lanes through classic Cheshire pastureland. Few villages are encountered but there are many isolated hamlets and interesting homesteads, some showing signs of conversion from chapels, water mills or schoolhouses. We visit Tilstone Bank and Bunbury Water Mill on the main arm of the Shropshire Union Canal, crossing the attractive Llangollan arm of the canal on our return.

Maps: OS Landranger 118 Stoke-on-Trent & Macclesfield and 117 Chester & Wrexham (GR 635577).

Starting point: The Venetian Village Marina car park. *By car:* from the A51 north of Nantwich take the unclassified road north signposted Wettenhall. The marina is on the left before the hump backed bridge. *By train:* Nantwich Station is less than ½ mile from the route. *By cycle:* from route 16.

Refreshments: At the Venetian Tea Rooms at the start and frequent pubs until Bunbury; then no facilities until the Pinfold Café close to the finish.

The route: Flat or very gently rolling lanes throughout.

Turn **R** out of the car park and over the canal bridge. Proceed through Cholmondeston to Wettonhall, passing the Little Man pub and the Boot and Slipper pub on the left. Take the next **turn L** (unsignposted). On many days of the year the roar of high powered motors can be heard across the fields ahead and the flash of racing cars or motor bikes glimpsed on the Oulton Park racing circuit.

Turn **L** (The Hall Lane – signposted Tilstone Fearnall) and before long again **turn L** (signposted Tilstone

Fearnall). **Turn L** at a T-junction (signposted Tilstone Fearnall) and soon, after the Crewe and Nantwich sign, **turn R** (Brains Lane – unsignposted). Take the first **turn R**, just past The Beeches, a new house, by a pond (Rookery Farm Road – unsignposted). Bear left, at an unmarked T-junction, to the main road where you go straight over the crossroads (village sign: Tilstone Fearnall).

Look right to view the Peckforton Hills on the skyline. Peckforton Castle is outlined clearly from this

Bunbury

angle and some of the ruined Beeston Castle can be discerned on the crag further right. The lane soon descends picturesque Tilstone Bank to cross the Shropshire Union main arm on a brick bridge. Here, note the old mill on the right, now a private house, and the lock and the little cone-shaped lock keeper's lobby on the left. In the early days all locks on the Shropshire Union had lobbies but increased traffic meant that more permanent lock cottages had to be provided instead.

Continue, climbing steadily over the railway, and over the crossroads (signposted Bunbury) to the T-junction opposite Bunbury church. Here the route continues to the right, but we **turn L** (signposted Bunbury Mill) and soon **turn R** (signposted Bunbury Mill) to view the mill. Retrace, passing the church of St Boniface on the left and the Dysart Arms on the right to enter Bunbury village on Vicarage Lane. Look right as you pass the three ways in the village centre to see the painted village sign.

Turn L at the T-junction by the Yew pub (Long Lane). Eventually the road bends sharp left by an old school house with a little spire. Here **turn R** (Cappers Lane). Go

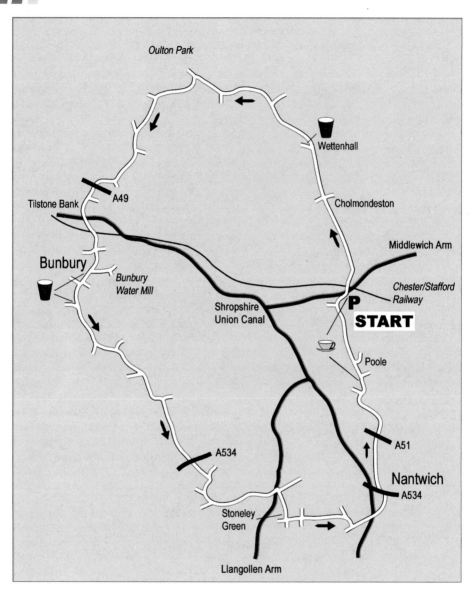

straight over the crossroads (Kidderton Lane) and **turn R** at the T-junction (Ikey Lane), soon **turn L** (Hollin Green Lane) and again at a T-junction **turn L** (unsignposted). Immediately after the Llangollen Canal **turn R** (Swanley Lane –

signposted Stoneley Green) and take the first **turn L** (opposite the Stoneley Green village sign, unsignposted). Go over the crossroads (Dig Lane) and **turn R** at the T-junction (unsignposted). Soon **turn L** at a T-junction

The Venetian Village Marina, near Nantwich

(unsignposted) and cross the main arm of the canal, keeping left on entering Nantwich outskirts and over some humps in a traffic calming area.

Turn L at the T-junction in Nantwich (signposted Wrenbury) and immediately before the aqueduct **turn R** (unsignposted), initially following the canal embankment. Eventually, the lane is signposted NCR 75 and Welshman's Lane. Go straight over the crossroads (Wettenhall Road), eventually passing the Metropolitan Knitting Centre with its Pinfold Café on the left. Here note the old stone pinfold (for penning stray cattle) on the left in the bungalow garden. Continue

through Poole to return to the marina, on the right before the canal bridge.

● ●

THE SHROPSHIRE UNION CANAL

This wonderfully wide canal is one of the last of the canal age, engineered by Thomas Telford utilising cuttings and embankments to keep locks to a minimum. It passes through some very rural little towns and beautiful countryside and is in fact not one single waterway but an amalgamation, which took place in 1846, of half a dozen separate companies. This ride begins at the Middlewich arm, which runs 10 miles from Barbridge Junction, on the Shropshire Union Main Line, to Wardle Lock, Middlewich, where it joins the Trent & Mersey Canal. We then cross both the main line and the Llangollen arm, which runs 46 miles from Hurleston Junction on the main line to Llantysilio Bridge, near Llangollen.

BUNBURY WATER MILL

First mentioned in 1290, then recorded in a survey of 1775, the mill was rebuilt c1850 and worked commercially, as a corn mill which augmented its income from local wheat by processing maize and cotton cake imported from America, until 1960 when a massive flood ended its working life. After years of decay it was fully restored by North West Water in 1977, as part of an ongoing programme of conservation and recreation, and is now a working museum. Information: 01829 261422.

BUNBURY CHURCH

There are records of a wooden Anglo-Saxon church and later a stone Norman church on the site; however, the present sandstone edifice dates from the 14th century when Sir Hugh de Calveley endowed a new collegiate church. In 1643 the church was fired by the Royalists and Victorian 'restorations' altered much of the interior. There was also damage from a landmine in 1940 but the whole is still a splendid sight externally. The tower, which stands on three fine Perpendicular arches within the nave and whose walls are nearly six feet thick, is founded on a sandstone outcrop and is strong enough to withstand the enormous stresses put upon it by the swinging of eight bells. Unlike many Cheshire churches, St Boniface's is usually kept locked.

NANTWICH

This charming market town, set beside the River Weaver, is one of the Wiches, the Cheshire 'salt' towns. Its fine medieval church, St Mary's, known as 'the Cathedral of South Cheshire', is surrounded by narrow winding streets with many Grade 1 listed timber-framed buildings. In Hospital Street there is Churche's Mansion, an Elizabethan merchant's house which survived the town's Great Fire and is now a restaurant, and also Sweetbriar Hall, a late 15th century timber-framed building. In High Street is The Queen's Aid House, which has an inscription on its panelling recording the support of Queen Elizabeth I in the rebuilding of the town after the fire, and also the Crown Hotel, built in 1585. Welsh Row and Wood Street are some of the oldest parts of town and here the Cheshire Cat was originally three cottages, built in 1637 and converted into almshouses, whilst at the end of Churchyardside are the elegant Dysart Buildings, a terrace of Georgian houses built in 1776. Salt is no longer produced in Nantwich but The Old Biot, the original salt spring with its many therapeutic uses, is preserved and provides brine for the outdoor swimming pool in summer. The town's museum on Pillory Street has displays that reveal the history of the town, together with a Cheshire cheese making room. Tourist Information: 01270 610983.

Beeston Castle, Bunbury and Cholmondeley Castle

18 miles

There are dozens of ancient, defensive castles dotted around the Welsh border but this route encompasses a fake since Cholmondeley 'Castle' is a product of the 19th century. However, that period's romantic inclinations have resulted in a splendid creation which many will prefer to the reality. The ride commences below the ruins of Beeston Castle, one of the genuine articles, and visits the peaceful village of Bunbury before taking to remote lanes past isolated farms and cottages. Approaching Cholmondeley Castle there is a single distant view of the castle and then a pleasant ride through the woodlands adjoining the deer park. The return is along the eastern flank of the Peckforton Hills where a series of paths may tempt you to park your bike and explore further on the Sandstone Trail for walkers.

Map: OS Landranger 117 Chester & Wrexham (GR 540590).

Starting point: Beeston Castle car park, opposite the castle gates (note evening closing time displayed). If you are not going to visit the castle you may be asked to use the nearby walkers' car park on busy weekends. *By car:* from the A49, south of Tarporley, turn west following signs to Beeston Castle. *By train:* there are no convenient stations. *By cycle:* from routes 15, 17, 18 and 20.

Refreshments: There are no cafés on this route but the Cholmondeley Arms and the Bickerton Poacher serve snacks and meals. At weekends and during school holidays there is usually a snack wagon in the Beeston walkers' car park.

The route: This is one of the easiest of rides, using almost entirely flat lanes, with slight climbs past Cholmondeley Castle and approaching the foot of the Peckforton Hills. There is about three-quarters of a mile of reasonably quiet A road.

Turn **L** out of the castle car park (unsignposted), passing the walkers' car park on the right and descending to the T-junction where you **turn L** (unsignposted). Very soon **turn L** at a T-junction (unsignposted), noting the attractive Beeston village sign on the right. Very soon **turn R** (signposted Bunbury). **Turn L** and **turn R** over the staggered crossroads (signposted Bunbury). In Bunbury village **turn R** at the T-junction (unsignposted), passing the fine Bunbury village sign on the left.

Beeston castle

Turn **L** at the T-junction by the Yew Tree pub (Long Lane, Spurstow – signposted Haughton). **Turn R** on the sharp left hand bend in the road (Cappers Lane – signposted Brindley), noting the unusual old house with its clock tower on the corner, to wind through pleasant pasture land.

Go straight over the crossroads (Kidderton Lane, unsignposted). **Turn R** at the T-junction (Whitehaven Lane – unsignposted). **Turn R** at the T-junction (Hollin Green Lane – signposted Larden Green) and very soon **turn L** (Hearns Lane – unsignposted). **Turn R** at the T-junction (signposted Chorley) and go through Chorley hamlet. **Turn R** at the T-junction (signposted Cholmondeley).

Go straight over the crossroads by the Cholmondeley Arms pub (Bickerton Road – signposted Egerton) to pass the entrance to Cholmondeley Gardens and the Deer Park Mere on the right, riding through pleasant mature woodlands with views of the castle grounds. Eventually, on the skyline ahead, the Larkton and Bickerton Hills appear to the left and the longer Raw Head, Bulkeley and Peckforton Hills to the right. Approaching Bickerton Hill, look out for Bickerton Hall on the left

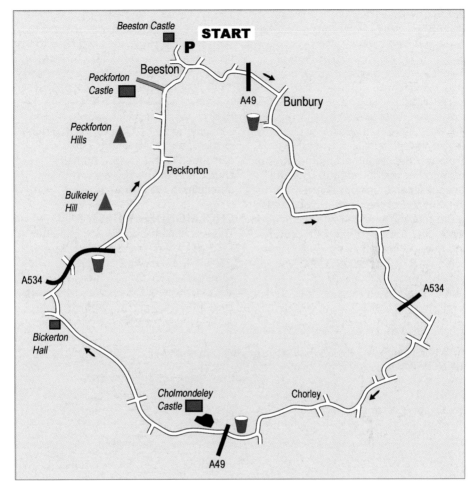

and **turn R** opposite (unsignposted, eventually signed Clay Lane). **Turn R** at the T-junction (unsignposted) and soon **turn R** at the T-junction (signposted Nantwich, A534). Take the second **turn L**, opposite the Bickerton Poacher pub (Stonehouse Lane – signposted Beeston).

Go through the hamlet of Peckforton, past a 'no through road' and the entrance to Peckforton Castle on the left and

then, for a short detour with a fine view of Beeston Castle, **turn L** as the woodland finishes (signposted bridleway) onto a tarmac lane with speed bumps. The best vantage point is in the vicinity of Moathouse Farm on the right. Retrace and continue. **Turn L** (signposted Beeston Castle) and immediately **turn R** (signposted Beeston Castle) to return to the car park opposite the castle gates.

BEESTON CASTLE

The 13th century ruin of Beeston Castle is a splendid landmark, located on a rocky summit 500 feet above the Cheshire Plain, facing the distant Welsh mountains. Originally a Bronze Age hill fort, the visible fortifications date from 1225 when a castle was built by Ranulf de Blundeville (1170–1232), based on new methods seen in the Middle East during the Crusades. The castle's strength centres on its imposing wall towers and powerful gatehouses and, unsurprisingly, it contains one of the deepest castle wells in the country. Beeston remained in good repair until the end of the 14th century and then declined until the Civil War in 1642, when it was brought back into commission and fell first to the Parliamentarians and then to the Royalists, after which it was destroyed. Beeston Crag and the castle ruins are in the care of English Heritage and there is a moderate admission fee. Information: 01829 260464.

BUNBURY

The church contains the remains, and an effigy, of the local hero, George Beeston, who was chosen as one of his company of pensioners by Henry VIII when he besieged Boulogne in 1544. He served similarly under Edward VI in the battle against the Scots at Musselburgh in 1547. Under Edward, Mary and Elizabeth, he took part in naval engagements as captain or vice-captain of the fleet. He was knighted for his part in the battle against the Spanish Armada, on board *The Ark*, at sea, by the Lord High Admiral in 1588. Remarkably he was reputed to be 89 years old at that time. In 1642 the 'Bunbury Convention', held in the church, declared the 'Neutrality of Cheshire' in the Civil War which unfortunately failed, the church being fired the following year. Nearby Beeston Hall suffered the same fate. On 19 March 1645 Prince Rupert dined with the lady of the house and, after dinner, told her that he was sorry but she should secure her valuables as he had to order the burning of the house to prevent its being garrisoned by the enemy. Bunbury church and the nearby water mill are described in the Nantwich route.

CHOLMONDELEY CASTLE,

This is a romantic gothic edifice built in 1801 of local red sandstone, set in a splendidly landscaped park with a mere. The rhododendrons which line the road are superb in season. To enter (the entrance by the mere) there is an admission charge, but the gardens are also very fine and there is a café. Information: 01829 720383.

THE SANDSTONE TRAIL

The original Sandstone Trail, officially opened in 1974, has recently been extended and now links the towns of Frodsham and Whitchurch. A tempting footpath leads from our route at the A534 to Raw Head, the highest point on the Trail, where the red cliffs, sculpted by the wind and the rain, are spectacular and the views to the west on a clear day are stunning. Copper was once mined in this area but production is no longer commercially viable. From Stonehouse Lane a path meets the Trail on Bulkeley Hill for excellent views eastwards to the Peak District and Cannock Chase and further paths cross the Peckforton Hills.

Beeston Castle, the Peckforton Hills and Overton Scar

23 miles

S tarting at a ruined border castle, this route explores a delightful little range of rich, red, sandstone hills in western Cheshire. Many of the lanes used are part of the Cheshire Cycleway and the National Heritage Byway and en route there are frequent striking views of Beeston and Peckforton Castles. The return is via the Cheshire Candle Workshops and over the Peckforton Hills.

Map: OS Landranger 117, Chester & Wrexham (GR 540590).

Starting point: Beeston Castle car park, opposite the castle gates (note evening closing time displayed). If you are not going to visit the castle you may be asked to use the nearby walkers' car park on busy weekends. *By car:* from the A49, south of Tarporley, turn west following signs to Beeston Castle. *By train:* there are no convenient stations. *By cycle:* from routes 16, 18, 19 and 20.

Refreshments: The Carden Arms in Tilston and the Cheshire Candle Workshops restaurant in Burwardsley.

The route: Almost all flat and gently rolling lanes, many of which are single track roads. One series of short, steep climbs to reach Higher Burwardsley and about ½ mile of firm unsealed and cobbled road with a steep descent which should be walked as it is designated a public footpath.

Turn **L** out of the castle car park, passing the walkers' car park on the right, and descend to the T-junction. **Turn R** (signposted Candle Workshops). When the road turns away from the woodland on the right, look back to view the splendid crag and castle. When the road turns sharp left, look left for views of both Beeston and Peckforton Castles, perched opposite each other on their respective hills. Pass the turn to the Cheshire Ice Cream Farm (worth a short detour – see route 20) and take the first **turn L** (Carrs Lane – signposted Cheshire Fishery).

The road bends sharp right in front of the fishery (a detour a few yards ahead offers views of the fly fishing from the car park). Continue round the bend. **Turn R** at the T-junction and immediately **turn L** (unsignposted, eventually signed

Dark Lane). **Turn L** at the T-junction opposite stone gateposts (Bolesworth Lane) to ascend gradually and take the first **turn R** (unsignposted) by woodland. Ascending gradually, with the grounds of Bolesworth Castle to the right, the lane cuts through a sandstone cliff before descending to the main road.

Go over the crossroads (Hill Lane – signposted Brown Knowl). **Turn R** at the T-junction (Hall Lane – signposted Duckington). **Turn L** at the T-junction in front of Broxton Old Hall (signposted Duckington). The road descends but watch for, and take, the first **turn R**, in front of a thatched, sandstone cottage (signposted Tilston, Cheshire Cycleway). **Turn R** at a fork and go straight over the A41 crossroads (signposted Tilston, Cheshire Cycleway).

Turn R at the T-junction in Tilston to the Carden Arms, the Cardens being the local landowners from the 14th century. **Turn L** at the crossroads in front of the Carden Arms, noting the stocks on the left (Church Road). Soon pass St Mary's church, then a Horton village sign, and then take the first **turn L** (signposted Chorlton).

If you enjoy rather odd and wild spots, detour a hundred yards to visit the striking red cliffs of Overton Scar. Look for a bridleway sign on the right as the road bends sharp left in front of a wooded rise.

Turn R onto this broad grassy track for about a hundred yards and, when the bridleway bends right, there is a footpath into the woods which hide the cliffs. Dismount to explore, then retrace to the road, where you **turn R** to continue.

Turn L at the T-junction and take the first **turn R** which is between two houses (unsignposted). **Turn R** at the T-junction (signposted Hampton) and soon **turn L** (signposted 'weight limit 17 tons') through woodland. Go over the crossroads (signposted as a single track road). Keep right at the fork by Lower Farm Court (signposted Cheshire Cycleway). Continue over the cross-roads (signposted Bickerton and the National Byway). **Turn L** at the crossroads by Bickerton church (Long Lane – signposted Broxton, Cheshire Cycleway).

Go over the cross-roads (signposted Harthill, Cheshire Cycleway). **Turn R** at the T-junction (signposted Cheshire Cycleway) and go through Harthill. On the descent **turn R** (signposted Burwardsley) and eventually take the first **turn R** (Church Road). Pass Burwardsley church and **turn R** at the T-junction. Climb steeply and take the first **turn R** (Barracks Lane - signposted Candle Workshops) and immediately **turn R** into the Workshops car park.

Leave the Workshops, taking the lane opposite the car park entrance. Soon, go straight over the crossroads

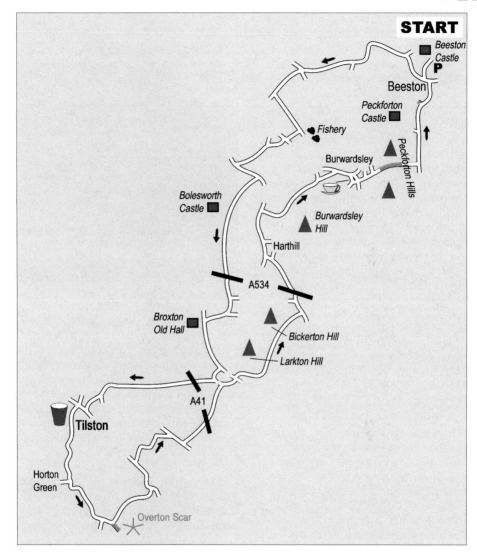

(signposted the National Byway, 'no through road') and ascend, keeping right at two forks. Past the Nantwich & Crewe Borough sign the road levels off, enters woodland and becomes unsealed, though firmly surfaced. After passing under a stone bridge the road becomes cobbled for several hundred yards and descends steeply before regaining tarmac. **Turn L** at the T-junction in front of a traditional Cheshire timber-framed cottage.

Pass the entrance to Peckforton Castle on the left. **Turn L** (signposted Beeston Castle) and immediately **turn R** (signposted

Beeston Castle) to return to the car park opposite the castle gates.

THE CHESHIRE CYCLEWAY

This is a well-signposted, 176 mile circuit of the county using quiet country lanes and well-surfaced sections of the Wirral Way and the Shropshire Union Canal, with specially designed cycle facilities for crossing some of the major roads. It is envisaged that the average rider could complete the route in five stages: Chester to Acton Bridge (45 miles), Acton Bridge to Bollington (35 miles), Bollington to Marton (20 miles), Marton to Malpas (43 miles) and Malpas to Chester (33 miles) but you can, of course, take as long or as short a time as you please. Leaflets are available from Tourist Information Centres in Cheshire. Further information on cycle routes in the county can be found at www.visit-cheshire.com or by telephoning the Cheshire Cycling Officer on 01244 603167.

PECKFORTON CASTLE

Built between 1844 and 1851 as a functional Victorian home with the style of a 12th century castle, on one of the few hills in Cheshire, Peckforton Castle is a ready-made location for film makers and has been used in a variety of productions, including *The Adventures of Sherlock Holmes*, particularly *The Boscombe Valley Mystery*, when the basement became a set of 19th century prison cells, and Doctor Who *The Time Warrior*, when Jon Pertwee as Doctor Who battled an evil Sontaran bent on conquering Mediaeval Olde Englande in and around Peckforton.

THE NATIONAL BYWAY

This is a 3,000 mile long leisure cycling route around Britain on lightly-trafficked rural lanes, with heritage sites its focus and

Beeston crag and castle ruins

rural regeneration its purpose. More than 500,000 heritage locations are recorded, ranging from hill forts to lost villages, historic woodlands, ruined castles and impressive stately homes. There are ruined monasteries and abbeys, and more than 12,000 churches which date from medieval times or before. The National Byway near Bickerton is part of the Malpas Loop and a sign explains that Bickerton means 'farmstead of the bee keepers' in Old English and indicates Larkton Hill with its Iron Age hill fort, Maiden Castle, which is accessible by footpath and offers views across the Dee Valley to Wales.

THE CHESHIRE WORKSHOPS

Entry is free to this little factory where you can watch skilled craftsmen and women carve candles by hand. Children can try their hand at making their own candles. There is a candle dipping ferris wheel, farmhouse kitchen, and other crafts on display. From the café there are fine views.

18

Malpas, Cholmondeley Castle, Wrenbury and Marbury

19 miles

This pleasant little route starts in gently rolling border country but, after skirting Cholmondeley Castle grounds, descends to the plain for a very easy ride through Wrenbury, visiting the Shropshire Union Canal and its famous lift bridge, and Marbury, with its leaning church by Big Mere, before climbing gradually back to Malpas on the lanes of the Cheshire Cycleway.

Map: OS Landranger 117 Chester & Wrexham (GR 486473).

Starting point: Malpas village car park. *By car:* from the A41, north of Whitchurch, take the B5395 to Malpas and a car park is signed on the right, before the post office. *By train:* start from Wrenbury Station, just off the route. *By cycle:* from routes 14, 16, 17 and 19

Refreshments: Cholmondeley Inn, the Dusty Miller in Wrenbury and the Swan Inn in Marbury.

The route: Just over a mile of B road on leaving Malpas and then lanes throughout.

Turn **R** out of the car park and very soon **turn R** (Chester Road – signposted Chester). Immediately after crossing a railway bridge **turn R** (unsignposted) and go straight over the crossroads (Cholmondeley Road – signposted Cholmondeley). The road climbs gradually, becoming a sunken lane bordered by sandy rabbit burrows, before levelling out with views of Larkton and Bickerton Hills to the left and then passing Hampton Springs Fishery on the right and the entrance to Egerton Lake Coarse Fishery on the left.

Turn **R** at the T-junction opposite the entrance to Cholmondeley Castle Kitchen Gardens (signposted Castle Gardens) to gradually descend through splendid mixed woodlands with views to the left of the deer park and mere. Pass the entrance to the castle gardens on the left and soon go straight over the crossroads (Wrenbury Road – signposted Chorley/Wrenbury) with the Cholmondeley Arms on the left.

After about 1½ miles, take the first **turn R** (signposted Norbury/

The lift bridge at Wrenbury

Swanwick Green) and then the first **turn L** onto a narrow lane (unsignposted). **Turn L** at the T-junction (signposted Wrenbury) and eventually the lane draws alongside the Shropshire Union Canal and the lift bridge appears ahead. **Turn R** at the T-junction and cross the bridge, passing the Dusty Miller pub on the right, the Cotton Arms on the left and soon, just before the church, **turn R** (New Road – signposted Marbury).

In Marbury, pass the Swan Inn on the right, noting the leaning church ahead. **Turn R** at the T-junction (Wirswall Road – signposted Wirswell/Bickley). For a closer look at St Martin's church and Big Mere **turn L** almost immediately. Otherwise continue on the winding lane. Go over the canal, eventually passing a turn to Swanwick Green on the right and then, soon after passing a fine black and white thatched house on the left, **turn R** (signposted Cheshire Cycleway).

The route now follows the well-signed Cheshire Cycleway as far as Malpas outskirts. Go straight over the crossroads (signposted Bickley Church/No Man's Heath). Approaching a T-junction, **turn R** onto a cycle path (signposted Cheshire Cycleway) and

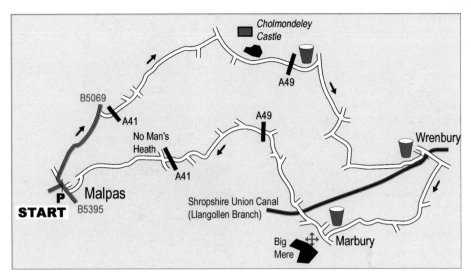

immediately **turn L** (signposted Cheshire Cycleway) to cross the busy A41. In No Man's Heath **turn R** and **turn L** over two mini-roundabouts (signposted Cheshire Cycleway, Malpas).

There is soon an attractive view of Malpas, perched on its little hill ahead. At the village outskirts, follow the one-way system, which takes a **turn L** (signposted Cheshire Cycleway, Wrexham), and at the T-junction **turn R** (signposted Bangor-is-y-Coed); go through the village centre, passing the Red Lion on the right and soon **turning R** into the car park.

• •

MALPAS

Lying in an area which was fought over for many centuries by the English and Welsh, Malpas is now an attractive little border village, part of a busy agricultural community, dealing mainly with dairy farming and the sale of hay and straw. Its main street, the B5069, is actually what remains of the old Roman road linking Chester with Wroxeter. A Norman castle was situated behind St Oswald's church and the mound on which it stood is still visible. St Oswald's, which dates from the 14th century, has late 15th and early 16th century additions. Inside can be seen some medieval stone carving, a 13th century iron bound oak chest, some interesting early stained glass windows and fine tomb effigies of the Cholmondeley and Brereton families. Other old buildings include the Market House, a 17th century tithe barn, the Cholmondeley almshouses built in 1721 and the Old School. The Red Lion Inn dates back to the 13th century and was once an important coaching inn on the London to Liverpool and Shrewsbury to Liverpool routes. The outside of the pub was 'modernised' in the 1920s, which hides the pub's age; however, the wood panelling is 13th century and a cut away section of the wall reveals the medieval daub and wattle framework.

WRENBURY

The Llangollen arm of the Shropshire Union Canal is the focus of interest in this sleepy village. It creates a constant stream of boats slipping through the lift bridge, believed to be one of only two such bridges in the UK that are open to road traffic. Uniquely, the River Weaver runs under the canal, through a Thomas Telford designed aqueduct to the rear of the Dusty Miller pub. At this point, the river once provided a millrace for the Dusty Miller building, which was a corn mill.

WRENBURY CHURCH

St Margaret's was built about 1500 from red Cheshire sandstone quarried in the Bickerton Hills. Part of the church was rebuilt in 1606, again in 1806 and was restored in 1865. Inside, the sandstone font dates from the end of the 16th century. The church is one of only nine in Cheshire to retain box pews; they were installed in 1608 and were originally four feet high but were reduced in height in the 1930s. The pew doors, added in the late 18th century, carry the arms of the families who owned them, mainly the Starkeys and Cottons, who were great rivals. In 1748 a dispute between the families was settled such that the Cotton family was allocated the south side and the Starkeys the north side of the chancel for their memorials. The church has a three decker Georgian pulpit and an unusual dog whipper's pew. In the churchyard, near the porch, is a remarkable cast iron gravestone dating from the middle of the 19th century.

MARBURY CHURCH

A church was first mentioned in Marbury in 1292, probably connected with nearby Combermere Abbey. The tower of

The leaning church of Marbury

St Michael and All Angels was built in about 1500 and has had problems with subsidence that probably date back to its original construction. The pulpit dates from the reign of Henry VII and is one of the oldest in Cheshire. Five of the six bells date from 1719 and the sixth from 1864. The clock was installed in 1849. The lychgate was built to commemorate those from the village who fell in the Great War. One of the newest features is the sun dial, set on the south wall as part of the Millennium celebrations. As at Rosetherne (route 5), the church overlooks a beautiful mere and the peaceful churchyard is an ideal spot to sit and watch for grebe and heron.

Malpas, Stretton, the Welsh Border and Sarn Bridge

18 miles

This ride starts out on a Roman road as far as the Carden Arms in Tilston, from where we turn north-east, to view Stretton Water Mill, before heading towards Wales, turning south just inside the border and riding parallel to the Dee Valley, across which there are views of the Welsh hills. The route slips over into Wales for just over ½ mile before the odd little village of Threapwood and then detours to meet the border again at Sarn Bridge, with its fine wooden water wheel on the Wych Brook. The return is through the isolated hamlet of Oldcastle Heath.

Map: OS Landranger 117 Chester & Wrexham (GR 486473).

Starting point: Malpas village car park. *By car:* from the A41, north of Whitchurch, take the B5395 to Malpas and a car park is signed on the right, before the post office. *By train:* Whitchurch Station is 6 miles to the south-east. *By cycle:* from routes 17, 18 and 20.

Refreshments: The Carden Arms in Tilston which is a popular cyclists' venue, the Bull Inn in Shocklach and the Queen's Head at Sarn Bridge.

The route: Apart from a few hundred yards of B road in Malpas, this ride is entirely on lanes and these are either flat or of a gentle gradient.

Turn R out of the car park (eventually signposted Tilston) to ride out of Malpas, noting the fine Old School House on the right. The lane runs straight, with just one detour around a hill, to Tilston. Here **turn R** in front of the Carden Arms (signposted Carden), before long passing the lovely Lower Carden Hall, almost hidden by its garden, on the right. **Turn L** in front of the massive gatehouse of what was once Carden Hall (signposted Stretton), eventually passing Stretton Water Mill, a little gem in an idyllic setting, on the left. On days when the mill is not working, it is still worth exploring.

At the T-junction **turn L** (unsignposted), passing Old Stretton Hall on the left, to soon **turn R** on a left hand bend (unsignposted). **Turn L** at a T-junction (signposted Shocklach) to ride south with the distant Welsh hills soon visible on the right. Go through Shocklach, passing a

89

The water wheel at Sarn Bridge

Millennium bench on the right and the Bull Inn on the left, and eventually take the **second turn L** (signposted Threapwood and Cheshire Cycleway). **Turn L** at a T-junction (signposted Threapwood) and, immediately after the Threapwood parish sign, **turn R** (Sarn Road – signposted Threapwood).

The route lies left, on Back Lane, but first continue, passing St John's church on the left, to Sarn Bridge, where the Welsh border runs along the lovely Wych Brook. Just across the bridge there is the interesting little Sarn Glass Studio, and on the English side is the Queen's Head pub whose attractive riverside terrace looks across the brook to an old water mill.

Retrace and **turn R** (Back Lane). **Turn R** at a T-junction (Sandy Lane) and immediately **turn R** at a T-junction (unsignposted, eventually signed Cheshire Cycleway). The lane winds past isolated farms and through the tiny (unsigned) hamlet of Oldcastle Heath. Approaching Malpas there are impressive views of the church across the fields. **Turn L** at the T-junction (signposted Cheshire Cycleway) through Malpas centre, passing the Red Lion Inn on the right, and **turn R** into the car park.

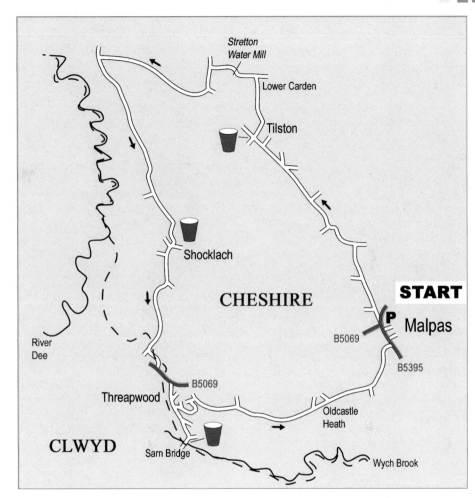

TILSTON

Dating back to Saxon times, Tilston comprises the four townships of Stretton, Carden, Horton and Grafton. The church of St Mary dates from the 14th century and in the churchyard the Hopley family tombstones have lines of verse on them, a Hopley having once been a poet. Nearby Carden Hall is described in route 20.

STRETTON WATER MILL

This small working water mill is set in remote and beautiful countryside. The four sets of stones are driven by an external overshot water wheel installed in 1777 (the flow of water is directed onto the top of the water wheel, which means it can use the weight of the water as well as the velocity and such water wheels are regarded as the most efficient) and a breastshot wheel dating from 1852 (the flow of water is directed at the level of the water wheel shaft, which means it can use some of the weight as well as the velocity of the water and such water wheels are regarded as the second most efficient). For a modest fee, the miller demonstrates

91

The old school house at Malpas

the whole skilled operation to transform grain into flour. There is an exhibition, a small shop and an attractive picnic area nearby. Information: 01606 41331.

SHOCKLACH
Nothing remains now of Shocklach Castle, but St Edith's church, Shocklach, seen to the west of the village about ½ mile from the River Dee, remains an attractive little Norman church and is well worth a visit. It is dedicated to St Edith of Polesworth, believed to be a sister of Edward the Elder, and was built by the local lord of the manor in about 1150. The nave is almost entirely 12th century, the chancel is 14th century, whilst the south door archway dates from about 1150 and is a good example Norman work.

THREAPWOOD
Until the early 19th century, when the rather severe-looking St John's church was built, this was an extra-parochial district, a tract of waste common land which was partly in Cheshire but chiefly in Flintshire, Wales. It was said to be occupied by characters of ill-repute, especially women of loose morals, who sought a haven there. The inhabitants were said to consider themselves beyond the reach of all legal authority. The county boundary was adjusted in favour of Cheshire in 1896 but the legacy of the village's outlaw past remains in the pleasingly unfocused and scattered pattern of the habitations.

Waverton, the Cheshire Ice Cream Farm and Stretton

28 miles

This ride starts out on some of the Cheshire Cycleway lanes alongside the Shropshire Union Canal, to then skirt the magnificent crag of Beeston Castle and visit the tea rooms at the Cheshire Ice Cream Farm. Continuing through charming Tattenhall village, the route heads south to idyllic little Stretton Water Mill and then swings west to Farndon on the Welsh border. The homeward run is via Churton, Bruera and Aldford on some of the quiet lanes used for the finishing circuit of the annual Mersey Roads Club 24 hour Road Ride.

Map: OS Landranger 117 Chester & Wrexham (GR 455642).

Starting point: Egg Bridge, Waverton, near Chester. *By car:* from the A41 south-east of Chester turn north-east onto Egg Bridge Road (signed Waverton) and the car park is on the right, before the bridge. *By train:* nearest station Chester, 4 miles. *By cycle:* from routes 16, 17, 19 and the Cheshire Cycleway.

Refreshments: The Cheshire Ice Cream Farm and the Shady Oak and Farndon Arms pubs.

The route: Almost entirely flat lanes with gentle climbs approaching Beeston Castle, Carden, the Barnston monument, and leaving the Dee Valley. About 2½ miles of quiet B road.

Turn **L** out of the car park and take the first **turn L** (Common Lane – signposted to the village hall), passing St Peter's church on the left and eventually following the course of the Shropshire Union Canal. **Turn L** (signposted Huxley, Cheshire Cycleway). **Turn R** at the T-junction in Huxley (Hoofield Lane – signposted Tiverton). As Beeston Castle begins to dominate the skyline to the right, **turn R** (Bates Mill Lane – signposted

Beeston), passing the Shady Oak pub on the left and crossing the canal and railway.

Ascend gradually, with splendid views ahead of Beeston Castle ruins, and **turn R** at the T-junction to skirt the crag. There is a fine vista to the right over the plain and, just before the next junction, through the trees to the left, high above is the closest view possible of the castle, without actually entering the grounds. **Turn R** at the T-junction (signposted Burwardsley), noting Peckforton Castle ahead. Eventually, **turn R** (Newton Lane – signposted Newton) and the Ice Cream Farm is on the left in about a mile.

Continue and **turn L** at the crossroads (Tattenhall Road – signposted Tattenhall). **Turn R** at the T-junction in Tattenhall (High Street – signposted Milton Green) and at the village outskirts **turn L** (initially signposted Harthill) for a gradual ascent. Go straight over the crossroads (signposted National Byway, Chowley Oak, Chowley Oak Lane). After just under 2 miles, **turn L** (unsignposted) in front of some new houses and almost immediately **turn L** and **turn R** over a staggered crossroads (signposted Carden village). The lane passes alongside hilly woodland to the left and a beautiful golf course in the grounds of Carden Hall to the right. Eventually, pass Higher Carden on the left and descend to **turn R** in front of a massive stone gatehouse (signposted Stretton), further descending to Stretton Water Mill, in about ½ mile on the left.

Continue and **turn L** at the T-junction (unsignposted), soon noting Old Stretton Hall on the left. Actually the adjacent Brandon House is the original 14th century timber-framed long hall and the present hall is an attractive 18th century country house. Soon

turn R (unsignposted). **Turn R** at the T-junction (signposted Farndon). Go straight over the crossroads (signposted Farndon) and soon **turn L** (signposted Farndon) into Farndon.

To view the packhorse bridge on the Welsh border, continue a few hundred yards down the main street. Otherwise **turn R** immediately before the Farndon Arms on the left (signposted Churton). The road ascends gently to the imposing Barnston monument on the left, where the plaque explains that Barnston served in the Crimean War and died following wounds received during the Indian Mutiny in 1857.

Continue through Churton, passing the White Horse pub on the left, and through Alford, where you **turn R** immediately after the bridge (signposted Bruera). Go through Bruera and Saighton. **Turn L** at a T-junction (this is a busy road and families may prefer to use the pavement on the left) and almost immediately **turn R** (Egg Bridge Lane – signposted Waverton) to return to Egg Bridge.

● ●

WAVERTON

Now picturesquely situated on the Shropshire Union Canal, this village has existed since Norman times. Its sandstone church with high tower, St Peter's, dates from Henry VII's reign; the carved wooden roof, font and at least one of the bells date from the 17th century.

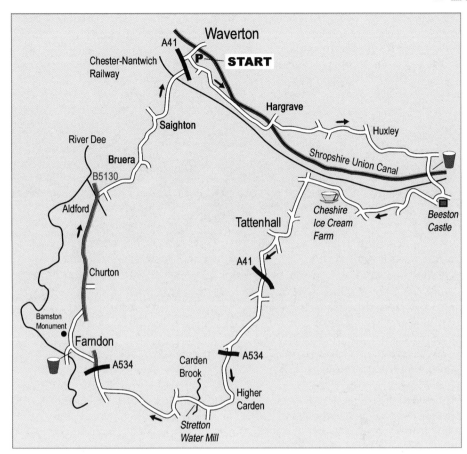

CHESHIRE ICE CREAM FARM

This is a working dairy farm, with rare breeds and pets, where you can watch the cows being milked. However, the main attraction is their café, which serves, in addition to morning coffee, light lunches and cream teas, over 30 flavours of ice cream. Admission is free. Information: 01829 770446.

TATTENHALL

The village is a delightful mixture of brick terraces, timber-framed cottages and beautiful oak-framed black and white buildings dating back to the early 16th century.

CARDEN PARK

Created by William Leche towards the end of the 18th century, the late 16th century Carden Hall was its focus. However, the hall burned down in 1912, only the cellars and landscape features surviving, and the park is now a golf course. In 1985 some Mesolithic flints were found in the opening of a rabbit burrow in the park and in 1996 the area was investigated thoroughly. An interesting aspect of the discovery was that the flints came from a mound of soil in front of a rock overhang, modified to form a small cave, which a hermit, John Harris, had occupied between 1744 and 1765.

Cyclists leaving Eggbridge car park

FARNDON

If you detour to view the packhorse bridge over the River Dee, which is the border with Wales, you might like to know that on stormy nights the banks of the river here are said to echo with the cries of drowning children. This alludes to the murder of the two sons of Prince Madoc by Roger Mortimer in the 14th century.

ALDFORD

The Roman road from Malpas crosses the River Dee here and a Norman called Richarde de Ald Ford built the castle, whose mound is visible to the north of the church, in 1160, but otherwise history seems to have passed by this attractive spot.

THE MERSEY ROADS CLUB 24 HOUR ROAD RIDE

On the last Sunday of July, between midday and about 3 o'clock in the afternoon, weary cyclists can be seen on this route between Bruera and Churton. They are on their way to Farndon Sports and Social Clubhouse to finish a 24 hour ride which has been organised annually since 1937, with a break during the war years. This Mersey RC 24 hour ride is the last remaining such to be held under the Road Time Trial Club rules and regulations.